PARENTS'
WORK
IS NEVER
DONE

PARENTS' WORK IS NEVER DONE

James M. Haines
and
Margery A. Neely

The cases presented are composites. No identification of actual persons, living or dead, is made in the case studies.

Library of Congress Cataloging-in-Publication Data

Haines, James M., 1945-
    Parents' work is never done.

    Includes index.
    1. Adult children--United States--Family relationships.
2. Parenting--United States. I. Neely, Margery A.
II. Title.
HQ799.97.U5H35   1986   306.8'74   86-33202
ISBN 0-88282-027-3

To Doris Elizabeth Neely Neil
who had the idea
and to our families

CONTENTS

PREFACE

The purpose of this book is to aid parents and professionals, as well as to counsel adult children from sixteen through thirty during periods of stress, and also to place such counsel in a framework of greater psychological growth. As spiritual, mental, and emotional problems beset grown children, the barriers to and strategies for "making lemonade out of a lemon" are important.

In addition to explorations of problems and solutions, a series of spirals are used to illustrate the difficulties and possibilities, since many people are visual and can understand points of discontinuity in the total context of their lives better if they can see those points as present moments in total years.

Never before in history have people lived so long. There are, therefore, no models of how older parents maintain meaningful attachment with their own maturing children. Never before has there been a period when so much centering on young children has resulted in so different a set of expectations by children. Grown children have new ideas about how much emotional, financial, and physical support they can demand from their parents. And never before have parents felt so confused as to the roles they should play.

Clearly, today's society in the Western world expects that parents' work is never done. This book will practically and theoretically guide that work toward freeing parents from unrealistic expectations and helping children from sixteen to thirty grow toward psychological well-being.

We express sincere appreciation to our families and to the many colleagues who have contributed to our psychological growth. Our thanks to Mary Hammel who contributed the fine artwork and to Linda Willis for the excellent typing. We also wish to acknowledge the fine assistance provided by Diane Iburg and by the editors, Joan Dunphy and Margaret Russell.

JMH & MAN

CHAPTER ONE

PARENTS EXCHANGE ONE SET OF PROBLEMS FOR ANOTHER

"My kids keep coming up with problems I have no experience in solving," complained Maria, a fifty-year-old statuesque brunette, at a bridge party.

"Yes, my pediatrician a long time ago told me parents merely exchange one set of problems for another as their children grow up. But, I agree that the difference is that our parents never had to deal with the things we do and, like you, I don't know how to handle them," said blonde and plump Bernice.

"What do you mean, problems are different?" Harriet challenged, running her fingers through her short, graying hair. "When growing up has always merely been children establishing their own independence and then parents, who want them to be independent, complaining when they're confronted with it."

"You're completely missing the point. It's not the adolescent stage I am talking about," rejoined Maria. "My children are in their early thirties, and they are the ones who keep turning up with stressful problems. They're still *dependent*, come to think of it. Yet, their lives include such a different set of experiences that we are truly from different eras." She tore a sheet from the bridge tablet. "Let's see what has happened that influenced them as they grew up that is different from our experiences growing up in the Depression and World War II." The other women leaned toward her and contributed ideas. When they finished they sat studying the list.

"Just look at these items. The events influencing today's young adults at critical points in their psychological development are mainly *social* issues, not the *sheer survival* issues we faced." Maria regarded them levelly with her clear gray eyes.

"Morality has changed: drugs, sleeping around, women working, space age, street violence, 'alternative lifestyles,' affluence, computers, now AIDS, terrorism," Bernice concluded. "I started out as a mother holding my kid while he took his bottle, which was a more human approach than the structured four-hour feeding my mother gave me and less close than the new return to breast feeding. For years my life was devoted to child-rearing. Maybe it was those new child-care methods that influenced the kids to try new things, to take on a larger moral responsibility for inhumanities, while they disre-

TABLE 1-1

SOCIETAL EVENTS INFLUENCING PERSPECTIVE

Major Events	Age	Child's Growth
1945–50 Peace, British Empire split, America world leader, atomic bomb, TV, no WW II destruction on North American continent, fathers back home, women retreat from workforce, consumer goods and education available to all, baby boom, readjustment era, Alan Nunn May, Igor Gouzenko	1–5	Born, fed, changed, held, talked to, walked, talked, loved, played, did chores
1951–55 Korean War, Cold War, McCarthy Era and Red Spy scare, affluence more widespread than ever before in history, U.S. Supreme Court rules on separate-but-equal case. Fuchs, Rosenbergs, Greenglass	6–10	Enter school, new friends, worked alone, with others read, write, did things outside family
1956–60 Great distances easily handled by auto or plane, family units spread out, Sputnik launched by Russia, great numbers of college grads educated under GI Bill enter workplace, popular buying of single-	11–15	Junior high, peers become important, skills developed, lots of clothes and toys

Major Events	Age	Child's Growth
family homes and appliances		
1961–65 Vietnam starting to be controversial, Bay of Pigs, Kennedy assassination, Space Age begins, War on Poverty in U.S., Peace Corps, VISTA, use of drugs widespread, Civil Rights Act passed	16–20	Enter high school, identity struggles, ideals become important, leave home, marry, college, work
1966–70 Civil Rights movement gathers momentum, draft card burning, fleeing U.S. to Canada, non-violent and violent disobedience of U.S. government, drugs held to be consciousness-expanding, hippies reject materialism, women storm workplace	21–25	Job, family, children born, dropped out, buy house, join clubs, join flower-children
1971–75 New morality with communes and living together, women's lib, the pill, vasectomies, great increase in single-parent households, "Me" generation, draft registration ended, some amnesty, Vietnam over, MIAs, Nixon resigned, Trudeau premier, inflation hits	26–30	Kids' expenses, search for meaning self/goals change

Major Events	*Age*	*Child's Growth*
1976–80		
Utilities and gas costs way up, recession-inflation staggering, latchkey children, world community at doorstep through media	31–35	One generation reaches middle age, the older one retirement
1981–		
Unemployment skyrockets, discouraged jobseekers, teenage pregnancies up, rape-domestic assault-child abuse statistics better reported and skyrocketing, inflation up and down, anti-nuclear demonstrations, jobs in low-paying service industries increase, microcomputers, divorce statistics at 50 percent, conservative tenor in government.	36–40	New generation reaches maturity; the cycle begins again

garded all our values relating to sex and drugs and being a good citizen. Maybe I paid too much attention to them. I feel guilty all the time. I want to protect them from problems they bring on themselves."

"Perhaps," Harriet mused. "I thought the way my husband refused to talk about his days in Vietnam actually conveyed that he hated war, how hatefully hellish war is. But something certainly taught the young certain conservative attitudes—my son is thinking of joining the military for a career!"

Serious-faced Joanie wrinkled her forehead,

"My daughter, who grew up in the seventies, did not take part in any of the marches or demonstrations. But every year when I think things have settled down, she or her family challenge me with some new problem. They keep bringing me into it. I've already raised her, I've paid my motherhood dues, and I resent the constant turmoil. Instead of civil disobedience, it's drinking and money and fights with her husband and the boss."

"Uh huh, I can remember," Bernice added, "when Barb was always talking about how she needed 'space' I was denying her. Now she's twenty-one it seems she's always invading *mine*. The advice she asks for and I give her, she doesn't accept anyway. I can't figure out her reasoning. She plays 'yes, but—' with me."

Middle-aged people in the 1980s are facing the trying dilemma of having to guide their adult children through issues with unknown, unfamiliar dimensions which seem to have no familiar link to their own experiences—and at a time when parents feel the children should be on their own. Often, when parents approach middle age or retirement age, it is with a sense of satisfaction with a life well spent, a job well done. Yet, although some values of their grown children are similar to their own, the range of problems and structure of right and wrong have changed.

The psychological growth that parents derived from adversity and peak experiences—such as job successes and failures, intact and disparate family life, birth and death—is, they feel, the fabric of life itself. Many grown children seem afraid of adversity. They keep coming back to the loom. They can thread their way through the problems of society, but not through their own personal problems.

How can a parent of adult children grasp the interwoven experiences and personal impacts such experiences make? How can the parent communicate fully with his adult child's experiential background? How can an understanding between parent and child be created out of the young adult's experiences?

Psychological growth as an adult is the constant movement toward wholeness through increasing:

1. awareness of personal characteristics

2. expenditure of serious effort

3. deliberate intention to meet change willingly

4. commitment to self and others.

Young people must feel secure or be committed to a larger purpose to grow and to become fully independent.

In order to assist the young adult in this quest and to grasp the personal impact and meaning of experiences, a parent has to listen to and consider the content of the situation within which the adult child finds him or herself, to recall his or her own similar reactions in situations that may have different context, but were also growth experiences. One's own experience can be metaphors for understanding the adult child.

Often the adult child keeps turning to the security of the parents because of the strong attachment between them. As the child senses the parents' support and their belief in the child's ability to make good decisions, he or she can move out to meet the challenge. Helping the blocked person review his or her own positive personal characteristics—as well as those barriers that cannot be changed—is useful. In order for children to become independent, they must expend the effort; they must feel that their actions will result in successful conclusions and that when they do not, the failures can be corrected so that the child can use the input from both successes and failures in future situations.

Communicating with the grown child involves positive active listening: Giving one's full attention, restating what the child says, identifying the child's underlying emotion or exploring what he or she feels. Isolating *why* the child feels so strongly is extremely helpful. Only after the adult child has a chance to describe and consider the problem and its ramifications can strengths, barriers, and alternative actions be discussed.

More serious problems—those beyond the parents' capabilities to discuss or explore—should be referred to a professional therapist. Rather than indicating that seeking professional help is a weakness or last resort, parents should provide strong support to the willingness to obtain it in order to meet the problem head-on and find ways to solve it.

Adult children, like their parents, have a propensity toward valuing certain experiences: loving their parents and using them as a secure base, developing work competencies, exploring, reaching toward social contacts, creating their own families, seeking physical release for tensions, believing in a higher cause, and gaining prestige. The particular context of these experiences differs among individuals, but the ability to share the meaning of such experiences is an essential growth mechanism. Psychological growth is the tendency toward integrated wholeness and mental, spiritual, and physical health. It is a predisposition toward self-actualizing experiences, such as involvement with the world, development of inner potential, feeling of serenity, desire for intimacy, seeking enjoyment, goal setting, showing respect for self and others, and expressions of appropriate emotions. This is what the grandparent generation called a *mature individual*.

The full range of psychological health, the various degrees of growth, occur when people are stretched. This expansion is represented in Figure *1-2* by the outer circle. The inner portion of the circle represents times of minimal growth. People who focus all their energy on sheer survival with no future orientation experience limited growth. Permanently institutionalized people might be limited or psychologically crippled in growth potential. However, the bulk of the population lies in the range experiencing enough psychological growth to learn more about themselves, to direct efforts toward a purpose, and to deal with change.

Some people benefit from growth workshops, others benefit when removed from day-to-day cares. Still others in dealing with those very same day-to-day cares.

The effect of the forces in a person's life on his or her psychological development at particular times, such as post-adolescence, can be represented as a spiral. As psychologist J. Purce indicated, a person's natural tendency is toward growth and

wholeness. Many parents believe, as did Shake-
speare, that growth comes from challenge: "Sweet
are the uses of adversity." But many young adults
taste adversity and find it is bitter.

Psychological growth experiences can also
pull one inward. These inward forces have an inhibiting or restricting effect whose nature and strength
vary.

Definitions of misfortune vary between generations. And while one can find perspective in looking
back, it is often lacking while one is undergoing the
"misfortune." How one defines *adversity* is of paramount importance: is it an opportunity to examine
goals and potential, is it threatening and depressing,
or has it aspects of both?

For example, some stimuli, such as technological advances, may affect different groups of individuals in different ways, especially those in the forma-
tive years of early adulthood versus the middle years.
The variance may be in the information known about
the technology (a rationally-based reaction) or in
perceived consequences based upon fear of the unknown (irrationally-based).

One person reacts with curiosity to robotics
because of the amount of information he or she knows
about its technology, and has a rational reaction:
"How can I use this?" Another person may have
irrational fears about the consequences, such as:
"Alien things will be running my life." A third, knowledgeable about technology's effect on employments
may have rational fears based upon estimated consequences that robots will replace human workers.
Sometimes these reactions are based upon individual

differences, but sometimes they seem rooted in one's age and life situation.

Technological advances can be restraining forces for one person and growth for another, which establishes an important point: the person having the experience interprets it subjectively. This point is especially important when one generation attempts to communicate with another. The maturing adult's subjective interpretation of experience influences his or her degree of psychological growth.

An individual's life experiences create his or her framework for interpreting the world. Thus, adult children have a different set of norms from their parents. Family life is a major influence on that interpretation.

The young adult often has difficulty conveying his or her feelings toward authority figures. Some ways of perceiving have individual meaning only and are hard to describe to another—especially to an older and more successful person. Yet, some mutual understanding is possible through common language.

Irrational beliefs can inhibit the growth toward wholeness. Analyzing the beliefs and offering new information and viewpoints helps.

In contrast, interacting with the world in a rational manner tends to promote outward growth. "Rational" is defined as "realistic" which also includes beliefs, emotion, and goals. Old interpretations and formerly-reliable solutions may have to be revised. Indeed, a childlike curiosity and sense of humor and wonder and delight are found in Abraham Maslow's self-actualizing people of all ages. As one perceives life accurately and interacts in a healthy manner, stimuli are interpreted as non-threatening, or at least controllable. In turn, one grows psychologically.

Other factors that influence growth opportunity may be: personal values, urban/rural setting, government policies, home, work, world and space events, religion, personal potential, and the values of one's ethnic group. Moreover, close personal relationships influence communication, love, warmth, and the degree of freedom one has to learn, explore and grow.

This list contains, also, every thought, event, experience, and stimuli that shape a person's psychological make-up. Growth over time does not occur in isolated humans. The child grows taller and fuller and attains puberty, becomes an adult, procreates, matures, notes physical decline. The particular genetic makeup of the human species allows for myriad adaptations through new learning to meet human challenges.

To illustrate the growth-restraining-opposing forces in the spiral, let's consider a child from an industrialized nation who has a caring and stimulating environment. Toys, television, music, art, science experiments, books, parents who converse and answer cues for caretaking, travel, and creative expression in the environment. The child's psychological growth has a *recurring* outward spiral.

On the other hand, a crowded, indifferent, impoverished environment, restricting and confining, would pull inward, and limit growth.

This illustration is generally—but not always—true. Certain people have experienced growth

Figure 1-1

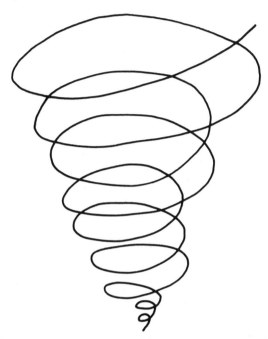

in restrictive environments or, although coming from a stimulating environment, have not grown. The key, of course, is how the individual reacts to and interprets events. Again, how the individual construes experiences is pivotal in understanding one's own children.

Another essential factor in psychological growth is the individual's ability to influence his environment. Thus, the interaction of people and environment is two way.

A person's self is the source of *willingness* and *intent*. To act on the environment, on beliefs and on events requires the will to do so. Whether the individual will act successfully depends upon how the experience is interpreted.

We can draw four guidelines from the interaction dynamics of psychological growth among maturing adults and their parents:

1. Young individuals have the ability to construe events in ways that are personally important but sometimes difficult to explain.
2. The individual with at least one secure, caring, *significant other* can feel free to move away and act.
3. The individual has the ability to monitor his/her own physical and psychological being.
4. An individual has the ability to act on the environment.

As we move away from the "me generation," we can thank that era for encouraging us to re-examine our goals so that there is deep personal meaning in attaining them. We hold personal values and more readily express emotions truly felt. This characteristic of young adults today adds different connotations to the definition of maturity than those held by earlier generations. Expressing irritation, anger, joy, or love is more openly encouraged. Self-sufficiency, seven-year-old autos, and Lamaze have become choices as acceptable as garbage compactors, golf, and face-lifts.

A person who perceives handling events as balancing factors between good and bad approaches the events with equanimity and confidence, or even anger-motivated action. He or she has sufficient self respect to be sensitive to the body's needs, views other people with interest and caring, and will progress through a period of psychological growth. So, adversity, as well as times of deliberate quest, are capable of building character.

The focus upon knowing oneself and questing after intrinsic awareness are not new discoveries. The basic Christian and Jewish doctrines were influenced by, and are taking new life from, some Eastern philosophies. The Golden Rule, the Ten Commandments, and the Judeo-Christian emphasis upon living an exemplary life on earth—the humane way human beings should behave toward themselves and others—reflect Confucian and Buddhist tenets.

Since the 1960s and 1970s Eastern philosophies have received new attention because they impart the idea that a sense of psychological development also concern spiritual being and awareness. Lack of awareness, cupidity, attachment, anger, arrogance, indecision, and opinionatedness are detrimental to such development. *Mind in Buddhist Psychology* calls these "six basic emotions which result in a restless mind." Contrast these emotions with eleven positive mental events: confidence, self respect, decorum, non-attachment, non-hatred, non-deludedness, diligence, alertness, concern, equanimity, and non-violence.

These positive mental attitudes can be used as resources in psychological growth in children from sixteen to thirty. Keep in mind, however, that potential growth toward the integration of them becomes difficult when obstacles arise. The list of obstacles to psychological growth (Table 1–2) will be discussed in subsequent chapters, along with the means of guiding. children in overcoming such obstacles. Even if

TABLE 1-2

**PSYCHOLOGICAL GROWTH OBSTACLES AND
RESOURCES IN MATURING ADULTS**

Obstacles	Resources
Sheer survival, grief	Diligence
Life-threatening situations	Self respect, alert examination
No motivation	Intent
Sadness	Cultivate inner potential
Poor interpersonal skills	Non-hatred, decorum, concern
Addiction	Break ritual
Spiritual unfulfillment	Equanimity
Focus on pleasure-seeking	Change attachment
Struggles with morality	Non-deludedness
Depression	Examination

the parent has little direct personal experiences to draw from, an analogy with *any* hoped-for goal *can* be made.

Look back at the influencing events (Table 1–2). In the 1950s, female parents devoted full attention to child care. They created a child-centered environment to a greater extent than ever before observed. In the 1960s and 1970s higher education and other institutions permitted changes demanded by young people as "relevant to life." Then the heady exercise of power and control by beloved and well-fed youth fell before revelations of the clay feet of government idols, ongoing reports of cruelty or violations of human rights, anarchy for anarchy's sake, demands of their own babies, who didn't respond to reason when hungry, shared parenting or career demands, recessions, and the stringent demands of living in a computer society.

And in times of both adversity and deliberate quest, grown children turn to parents to "kiss away the pain."

The problems which obstruct psychological growth are numerous. The young adults who are our children seem to feel cheated, yet we often as parents feel there is no more we could have given them psychologically. We did our best. Why, then, do we feel guilty? Why are we continually being emotionally drawn into situations that we never would have thought to ask *our* parents to handle after *we* reached adulthood?

If the psychological growth of our children can be defined as growing toward wholeness, health, and utilization of potential, then the definitions of these elements must hold the solutions. If growth is hampered by lack of goals or violated movement toward defined goals, children want and need our help in providing direction.

The young adult experiencing the barriers of depression naturally turns to the strength of the parent who has made it through similar periods. Indeed, the need to re-affirm parental support typical of an earlier stage of the child's life is natural. They feel we can help them figure out how to move through, around, or stand-off the obstacle causing their "lows"—as we have in the past. And, many times indeed, we can help them contain the problem and expand flow in other directions.

If our spiritual experiences, the environment, the world, morality and values, and interpersonal relationships have provided signposts, then we can assist our children by reviewing our own past. People do have somewhat similar stages of growth, although the goals of individual men and women may differ. The past can be a guide to the present, even though the old familiar maps of the countryside of life may need new interstate highways that get our grown children to the same place we are: maturity. But we, as older adults, need to know "where they [our children] are coming from" in order to help them get to where they want to go.

CHAPTER TWO

COMMUNICA-TION BETWEEN GENERATIONS: SPOKEN AND UNSPOKEN

"Last week we discussed issues relating to communication. As an assignment each of you was asked to study the interaction between the members of your families," opened the facilitator of the parent group.

"This past week my husband and I took our son, Billy, to visit my parents. In light of what we'd been talking about in this course it was a real eye opener," stated Tracy Bronski. "My father greeted our son with the usual, 'How many girlfriends do you have?' It was obvious to everyone but my parents that Billy was embarrassed."

"It was interesting to watch my parents interact with our children on the weekend visit," interjected Terry Tomkins. "Since my divorce they've seemed unsure what to say to the children. They didn't say much, but they did ask the kids to sit next to them and also on their laps. The children really seemed to sense a love and caring that was being transferred without saying much. Now that I think about it my ex and I didn't do much of that kind of holding."

"I feel the most significant interaction this past week occurred between my sixteen year old daughter and myself. In an earlier session we discussed minimizing the advice we give and talked about allowing our children space to solve their own problems," added Jackie Rodriguez. "Being a single parent requires the cooperation of all members of the family. Well, laundry did not get done as quickly as it should have. My daughter came into the kitchen quite upset that there weren't any dry panties for her. They were still on the line. She tried to get me involved and give me ownership of her problem. I listened as best I could—and counted to ten. She stormed out angry because I wasn't going to leave meal preparation to meet her immediate needs. After a few minutes I wondered what had happened so I quietly tiptoed to her bedroom. There she was on the floor with the hair dryer drying her panties. Talk about solving your own problems! What's better I avoided the stress of trying to solve it for her."

"The first one I want to mention happened in the supermarket," said Evelyn Reinhold. "A mother had an infant in a cart and a toddler walking beside her. The toddler reached out toward the grapes. The mother quickly swatted his hand down. With obvious hurt in his voice, the boy asked, 'Am I a bad boy, Mommy?' The mother snapped back 'Yes.' I could see the boy withdraw into himself. Last week we discussed that the person may be fine, but the act is the thing that is unacceptable. The entire incident left me with an emptiness in my stomach."

Through involvement in parent groups such as the one demonstrated above, an increasing number of parents are exploring the communication patterns between their maturing children and themselves. Further understanding of communication may improve and enrich these relationships.

As we know, change often isn't easily accomplished. Just as we would like our grown children to change some of their behaviors, we must be willing to examine and consider alternative communication styles. A key point to remember is that modelling is important in promoting change in others. Even though people may view the way in which they communicate with others as acceptable, a critical first step to change is a willingness to undergo self examination.

It can be safely assumed from the example above that Tracy Bronski's father didn't mean any harm by greeting his grandson with the question, "How many girlfriends do you have?" The issue is whether other greetings would have better promoted and developed the relationship between them. The purpose of this chapter is to examine communication patterns, both verbal and nonverbal. A goal is to provide a vehicle for communicating more accurately and developing closer relationships.

Individuals considering change need to acknowledge that some methods of communicating could be improved. In another chapter we bring up the case involving Bill Williams, who had the second job, as an example of the importance of being open to consider change. Were Bill unwilling to evaluate the impact that the job was having on his family, chances for improved marital and family relationships would be greatly reduced.

Such is also the case with improving communication. Individuals are usually comfortable with their patterns of relating to others. Quite possibly no one has confronted them with the idea that their methods of dealing with others could be improved. Some patterns, such as humor, are rarely viewed as limiting relationship building yet they may actually harm relationships.

The use of humor is frequently seen as harmless, and often it is. There is a need to laugh and see the lighter side of life in everyday situations. Laughter provides a valuable break from daily routines, frustrations at work, and the life-threatening focus of the news media. Just as a balanced diet promotes better health, humor offers relief from the stress of high-tech life styles. However, in some individuals humor is not balanced by serious conversations which acknowledge the wide range of emotions generated within each of us. As such, humor-laden conversations often lack a balance.

Humor may be perceived as being insensitive. The opportunities to promote deeper, more meaningful relationships are often missed without the ability to converse at a variety of feeling levels. For example, the greeting of Tracy Bronski's father, at the beginning of this chapter, was meant to transmit a warm welcome. But the question may be raised whether alternatives could have conveyed these feelings more accurately. This is not to imply that humor has little place in the interaction process between children and their grandparents. Laughter between children and adults serves a valuable purpose. Humor can convey warmth for some children. For others a more direct expression is necessary. From time to time children, both young and grown, wonder whether significant adults really care for or love them. It is often hard for some parents to recall the last time that they expressed directly to their children, young or grown, such messages of caring as "I love you," or "I'm proud of the way in which you've gone out and looked for a job."

As a society we have not been encouraged to send messages of affection. Even at a distance, such as in phone conversations with loved ones, the words "I love you" are sometimes virtually impossible to force out. Tracy's father may be one person who finds it very difficult to express warm feelings toward his children and grandchildren. He may well be one of the many people in whom expressions of warmth between human beings was never encouraged. Instead of greeting his grandson with the question "How many girlfriends do you have?" he could more accurately have welcomed him with a direct statement such as "I'm really glad to see you again." Such a statement is reasonably simple, and a true reflection of the feelings the grandfather may wish to convey.

For someone raised in a family where the adult models didn't value an expression of feelings, changes could prove extremely stressful. While females have found it socially acceptable to cry and, in general, to be more expressive of what is affecting them, verbal acknowledgement of caring, for men in particular, hasn't been valued.

A primary drawback with the use of humor is that all people don't perceive a humorous comment in the same way. The following is a case in point:

INTERACTION #1

Susan: "I hate summer. Freckles make people look like spotted leopards with sunburns, and I have a million."

Mary: "I think freckles can be a sign of beauty."

Craig: "Yeah. If you get enough of them you look tanned."

Susan is attempting to convey a feeling of dislike for the freckles she has. Mary's response is generated by her own defense mechanism since she has freckles also. Whether Susan believes Mary or not is another issue. The point is that Mary didn't perceive Susan's anxiety about her own looks. Instead, Mary understood the remark to be directed toward her. The possible negative results of such a remark are obvious.

Although Craig's response may not have been intended as being directly hurtful, the reinforcement of the anxiety could be almost as devastating. Craig's response may have not intended to hurt at all. However, his humor may have reinforced both Susan's expressed fear and Mary's subconscious one that freckles are ugly. Due to the unintended ways in which humor can be received, it can be a very danger-ous method of communicating, particularly on serious emotion-laden subjects. Interjecting humor into a serious conversation may be an avoidance technique. Rather than participate in an emotionally charged conversation, some people either withdraw or change the subject through the use of humor. For others, such as Craig, humor may constitute the majority of his verbal interactions.

The dialogue above and possible message which correspond with each could have been:

INTERACTION #2

DIALOGUE	*MESSAGE*
Susan: "I hate Summer. Freckles make people look like spotted leopards with sunburns and I have a million."	Concern over how her peers may view her looks during the summer months.
Mary: "Recently there was an article in a movie magazine about stars who have freckles."	Attempt to normalize freckles and to reassure Susan that people with freckles can be considered attractive.
Craig: "I've know you for years and haven't noticed your freckles."	An attempt to reassure Susan that her freckles are not as obvious as she may feel.

The fact that Craig has responded less negatively does not mean that Susan will accept his statement at face value. However, she does have the opportunity to take it at face value. He could have just as easily followed Mary's movie-star comment with "Yeah, the freckled stars always get the roles of the monsters." Responses such as this cross over the line from humor to hurtful sarcasm. Sarcastic responses contain a bitter, more openly hurtful tone. In addition to the avoidance element, the contemptuous challenge contains an obvious lack of sensitivity.

In addition to the use of humor and sarcasm, labelling can also have a similar effect of failing to promote personal growth and relationship building. The following dialogue provides an illustration.

INTERACTION #3

DIALOGUE	*MESSAGE*
Grandson: "I don't like onions. Are there onions in this salad?"	An honest straight forward message, possibly based on fact.
Grandmother: "Yes, there are. They're good for you. Now eat them up."	Honest response but the directiveness in the third sentence has a ring of authoritarianism and power.
Grandson: "They give me a stomach ache." (Starting to whine)	Providing justifiable reason why he shouldn't eat the onions.
Grandmother: "Now stop acting like a baby. You're a big boy and only babies act like that. Eat a little. I know you'll like it."	The labelling provides a stigma which is not productive to resolving the situation. The statement that the child will like it falls on deaf ears and discredits the grandmother.

Labels such as "baby," "suck" and "fool" are of no use in promoting psychological growth toward responsible behavior. With grown children the labels may change but the hurt and counterproductive nature remains basically the same. A danger is that those being labeled may resign themselves to such labels. In such cases the method to achieve the goal may turn out to have just the opposite effect. In the example above the grandmother took a stand which provided little opportunity for either adult or child to withdraw from gracefully. A similar stituation develops below in a conversation between a parent and her twenty-three-year-old son.

INTERACTION #4

DIALOGUE	*MESSAGE*
Son: "I'm going to buy a new sports car."	Possibly an invitation to discuss the issue rather than making a definitive statement.
Parent: "What do you mean you're going to buy a sports car? You sound like a sixteen-year-old."	The confrontation and labeling begins to close the possibility for further conversion.
Son: "No. This is the last time I may be able to. In another few years I could be married."	Offering a reason for the purchase and possibly still wanting to discuss the purchase.
Parent: "You'll never learn. You spend money like a drunken sailor!"	Further labeling and no expression of willingness to talk.
Son: "I earn it. I can spend it."	Abruptness and confrontional style developing.

Parent: "You're just a parasite. Still living at home. If you think you can afford a better car than your parents, then you should be paying more rent."	More labeling and bringing up subjects which might be better discussed at a more appropriate time.

The escalation of this confrontation is apparent. The labeling by the parent is not productive. In fact this exchange may well be counterproductive.
The son may pursue the purchase in an attempt to prove the parent wrong. And, if frustration or failure follows then the son may develop an insecure attitude, "You were right, I am no good and I will continue living up to your expectation." Once this negative self-scenario begins it takes much skill and counseling to reverse it. The dialogue below demonstrates an alternative path that the above conversation could have taken.

INTERACTION #5

DIALOGUE	*MESSAGE*
Son: "I'm going to buy a new sports car."	Despite the fact that the statement is emphatic, there may be room for discussion.
Parent: "This is the first time you've mentioned a new car, and a sports car in particular."	Response is nonjudgmental and provides an invitation for further discussion with a statement that asks for more explanation without being too confrontive.

Son: "Well, I was thinking that in a few years I'll be married and a sports car may not be suitable. It's something that I have always wanted."

Presenting a rationale for the purchase yet there is still opportunity for further discussion.

Parent: "Several of your friends have sharp cars and I imagine that you'd like one too. On the other hand, we haven't been charging you much rent in order to help get your feet on the ground. If you feel that you have extra money, then we should also take a look at you paying more for your room and board."

The parent demonstrates some understanding why the son may wish to make the purchase, but at the same time without any name-calling or labeling confronts the son on the issue of the rent.

Son: "Well, if I pay more rent I won't have the money for the car."

The son has admitted the dilemma which he is faced with. This now leaves both parent and son with the task of negotiating the conditions of sharing future financial expenditures.

Not all interactions between parents and maturing children go so smoothly. By avoiding negative comments, though, satisfactory resolutions are more likely. Without the use of labeling there is an improved chance that both parties may have their needs met. The negative effects of statements using humor, sarcasm, and labels are quite obvious when compared with other forms of communication.

As with humor, there are occasions when agreeing or praising have the effect of building a relationship. However, when used too frequently or inappropriately, the sound is hollow, lacking a sincere quality. A marginal example was offered by Mary in the freckle example. Mary's statement "I think freckles are a sign of beauty," although not meant to be destructive, may not help someone who perceives his or her freckles to be a sign of ugliness, as does Susan. Examples of hollow acclaim abound.

INTERACTION #6

Daughter: "I filled out an application form for a job at City Hall. I hope I get the job."

This daughter is expressing pride at taking her first step toward getting a job. There is also an expressed hope that the result will be positive. She may also be apprehensive as to how this will turn out.

INAPPROPRIATE RESPONSE	MORE APPROPRIATE RESPONSE
Parent: "I'm sure you will."	"I admire your initiative in going out to apply for the job. It's not always easy."

Unless there is a reason for such a firm statement, the hollowness of the inappropriate response is obvious. By responding in such a manner the parent demonstrates poor judgment or a lack of knowledge of how the world operates. This brings into question the parent's ability to provide reliable opinions. Furthermore, the daughter is built up in anticipation for being offered the job. A negative response from City Hall will be that much more difficult to accept and keep in proper perspective.

The more appropriate response would show that the parent shares feelings of pride in the daughter's willingness to face stress and possible rejection by applying for a job. The parent further acknowledges that it isn't easy to tackle the realities of job searching. Through this parental response the daughter would be reassured that some of the feelings of apprehension she is feeling are normal and that the parent does in fact understand. The parent keeps her response short. This allows the daughter to respond further with other possible concerns or thoughts she may have.

INTERACTION #7

Ten-year-old Granddaughter: "Grandma, I would like to be Miss Teen:"

There are a wide variety of reasons why a ten-year-old may make this statement. One is that she may be seeking possible confirmation as to her own physical appearance. In this society looks and social acceptance are still issues of concern for many females. The granddaughter may be expressing admiration for the physical appearance and possibly the talents of those women who appear on the television. An underlying issue may well be that the ten-year-old's mother is questioning the appropriateness of the role models offered by the Miss Teen contestants. Such beauty queens are under increasing attack from sources who view such contests as an exploitation of women. For young females this conflict in values often confuses them as to the appropriate roles to pursue.

INAPPROPRIATE RESPONSE	*MORE APPROPRIATE RESPONSE*
Grandmother: "If you want to, you can."	"It must be hard work to become Miss Teen. They have all worked hard to develop talents."

The grandmother's inappropriate response was well intentioned. She wants the best for her grandchild and hopes to encourage her to pursue goals. However, the reality is that just because the granddaughter wants to become Miss Teen doesn't mean she can. Such a response fails to acknowledge the difficulties and hard work involved in becoming Miss Teen. Many people become easily frustrated when faced with life and the fact that wishing or wanting doesn't make it so. Just because someone wishes to keep a marriage intact doesn't guarantee that it will remain so.

By beginning to present some related issues to becoming Miss Teen, the grandmother's more appropriate response begins to prepare the child for life. Just because most don't become the queen doesn't mean that they can't be happy and successful. By making the ten-year-old aware that people can combine goals such as attending a university and competing in beauty pageants, the grandparent could provide valuable information. Furthermore, the grandparent has not reinforced unrealistic goals which have an extremely low probability of being achieved.

Humor, sarcasm, labeling and praise/agreement are only a few of the communication styles which are potentially laden with negative effects on the psychological well-being of maturing children. Further examples of inappropriate responses are provided in Interactions 8, 9 and 10.

Ideally, responses should encourage the grown child to satisfactorily resolve his situation. This process is often accomplished by providing a forum to discuss openly their feelings and explore a range of issues and alternatives involved. Responses which do not promote this process to a satisfactory conclusion do not provide the grown child with an opportunity for psychological growth toward becoming a responsible independent individual, capable of resolving his or her problems.

INTERACTION #8

Male Grown Child: "I was the best qualified person for the job. I should have gotten the promotion. I know more than that college graduate and a woman at that."

POSSIBLE PARENTAL RESPONSES

Humor: "Have you heard the current saying? The best man for the job is a woman."

Sarcasm: "You'd think that your boss would know a high school graduate is better qualified than a college graduate."

Labeling: "That's the problem with you young punks. You're too damn lazy to spend your time working your way up."

Agreement: "You're right. Your company will live to regret this decision."

Advice: "You should consider looking for another job."

Lecturing: "Now let's get one thing clear, life is not going to hand you advancement on a platter. You've got to learn to live with setbacks. With hard work you'll be able to prove yourself worthy of the next promotion."

Cajoling: "Come on now don't get down. Look on the positive side, tomorrow is a new day."

Avoidance: "I refuse to discuss such negative views. Don't try to draw me into a talk about the relationship between you and your boss."

Threat: "If you don't get a promotion and start making more money soon you'll never be able to afford to get married.

POSITIVE ALTERNATIVE: "I know you were hoping to get this job. You must be discouraged to have been turned down."

INTERACTION #9

Twenty-two year old son, living at home: "I'm finding that I am having trouble making ends meet this month. I was wondering if you could lend me enough money to get me to the end. Also, I need another $100 to reserve a spot for the trip to Florida next month."

POSSIBLE PARENTAL RESPONSES

Humor: "Are you in training to be a comedian? Or do you figure that I won a lottery?"

Sarcasm: "You've been reading so many Richie Rich comic books that you've lost touch with reality."

Agreement: "Sure. Money is tight for me but I'll get by somehow. I could always borrow it."

Lecturing: "How many times do we have to go through this speech about budgeting and financial planning? You aren't handling your money very well. What I'm willing to do is sit down with you and analyze every cent you earn to create a surplus."

Cajoling: "Let's sit down and talk as friends. Surely, your finances aren't as bad as they seem."

Avoidance: "As a mater of fact I wanted to talk with you about how much gas you've been using in the car lately."

Threat: "I'm sick and tired of you asking me for money. If you don't get this money matter under control, I'm going to take control of your pay like I used to when you were sixteen."

POSITIVE ALTERNATIVE: "I wasn't aware that you were this tight for money. It sounds like you're in a bind."

INTERACTION #10

Grown Daughter: "I've decided to leave Bill and file for a divorce."

POSSIBLE PARENTAL RESPONSES

Humor: "Go for the camper. We'd like to borrow it next summer."

Sarcasm: "I know he's not good for much, but at your age it may be tough finding anyone any better."

Labeling: "I know he's a no-good, but you've always been a hot-head, making quick decisions."

Agreement: "Sounds like you're making a wise decision."

Advice: "If I were you, I'd see a lawyer, just to make sure you get your fifty percent."

Lecturing: "This is a very complex matter. I hope you've thought it over sufficiently. Many people rush from one situation to another and regret it. You should weigh it carefully. Your mother and I could have separated many times, but we stuck with it."

Cajoling: "Oh, come on now. Things can't be that bad. After all he's a hard worker and a good provider."

Avoidance: "Are you aware of the problems your mother and I have had lately?"

Threat: "If you do that, don't plan on moving back here."

POSITIVE ALTERNATIVE: "You sound like you've made your mind up for sure."

In Interaction 10, the parental advice to consult with a lawyer is sound. However, through the process of discussing the issues involved it is hoped that the daughter would arrive at this decision herself. In doing so she would, it is hoped, develop a feeling of self confidence as a person who can better resolve future problems when a parent isn't there.

Similarly, the three agreement responses have a note of finality. With an authoritarian ring to each, the parent fails to encourage further discussion. For example, assuming that a lengthy discussion has not previously occurred regarding whether the daughter should divorce her husband, the parent may be better to encourage an evaluation of the pros and cons. Implications are often overlooked. Other response styles, such as lecturing, cajoling, avoiding or threatening, have similar weaknesses.

The main point is that communication patterns do have an impact on personal relationships and promoting psychological growth. A variety of patterns are healthy and necessary in developing a well rounded person. Such people are generally more in touch with their range of feelings and are able to express them. The issue is not whether a variety of styles should be used, but rather using them at appropriate times. Some families may appear to use inappropriate verbal interactions patterns and still have children with adequate psychological growth. For these families balanced interactions patterns may exist in other forms. Often a strong relationship was developed between parent and child during the early years of life. For an individual with a good self-image, the impact of some negative comments may be considerably less when compared with the person who has a negative self-image. Families whose children have good psychological balance are often used as examples to point out that there is nothing wrong with the use of periodic inappropriate parenting techniques. For them the damage is less obvious and more easily recovered from because of the other positive aspects to their relationships, both verbal and non-verbal, from the past and the present.

However, for individuals with limited psychological growth poor verbal interaction may have a devastating effect. The result may be a feeling of helplessness, a damaged self-esteem, and ultimately a chronic state of depression.

CHAPTER THREE

YOUR CHILDREN'S MARITAL PROBLEMS

Darcy and Darin Holt were talking to some friends at the Senior Center luncheon. "Our son—he's thirty-eight—called last night. Last month his wife left him a note that she was tired of being a housemaid and was leaving him and the three kids. Yesterday he was served with divorce papers. George has been frantically trying to find babysitters for the eight-year-old twins and ten-year-old Mary. I think he wants us to take the kids. We don't know what to do."

"You are in the same quandary we are," said Henry Murdock, gesturing toward his wife Pam. "Our Carolyn had not been writing, so last week we drove down to Philly to surprise her with a visit. She had a black eye, a small cut by her lip, and the five-year-old cried when I swung him up by the arms. Bruises. Crisis center. But she's afraid to leave. She's nearly twenty-five years old and has no job. If we encourage her, then she may want to move in with us. She was only eighteen when she ran off and married without asking us."

Picture the Murdocks' daughter, Carolyn, being afraid. Did you see a person showing only visible signs of fear? Or, did you also see something that was causing her fear, or did you add some meaning of your own for the cause of fear?

Picture the Holts' son with his three children. Did you only imagine the foursome, or did you add inferences as to the amount of physical labor and frustration you might experience in a similar circumstance?

The past experiences of one person have to be described to another. Otherwise, the other person may be interpreting the experiences only in terms of his or her own personally limited structure of meaning attached to such events. Yet, one experience forms the basis of other interpretations.

A person's past and future psychological space is parallel to the time line. As the past experiences are drawn upon to project understanding or future movement, the actual passage of time becomes unimportant. Experiences from the past form the bases for estimates that a person makes about the present and future and how feasible new solutions might be.

People take in their experiences through their senses and assimilate them into their psychological makeups. The eyes respond to stimuli that are then interpreted by and stowed away within the brain. Visual reconstruction of events is possible through the phenomenon we call the "mind's eye." We can also visually construct new events out of that tucked-away information.

We can recall bits of the alphabet or a song by replaying the mental tape of those aural memories. We can hear a "little voice" admonishing us not to do certain things. Our "little voice" stems from adult admonishment. Touch and emotions and movement may evoke treasured memories. The smell of a diesel engine reminds us of a trip on a tramp steamer; the smell of a rose, a romantic dance. We feel patriotic when the national anthem plays. A glass of cold cider in January reminds us of autumn sun, and the taste of burnt marshmallows takes us back to a campfire.

Repeated kinesthetic feedback enables us to find the keyhole in the dark, to find the light switch. Balance lets us maneuver slippery walks, negotiate steps we tumbled down as infants. The "sixth sense" of intuition (which may be the "seventh") lets us move a glass of milk perched on a perilous ledge before it is knocked over.

So the senses that take in events also evoke memories of earlier events. The representation of these events in our interpretations has been called a person's "deep structure" by John Bandler and Richard Grinder in their two-volume work, *The Structure of Magic*. Bandler and Grinder noted that people in therapy were helped most by therapists who had been able to get the patients to describe their deep structures.

A person who says to the therapist, "I'm afraid," leaves several questions unanswered. The therapist has to ask, "You're afraid of what? How are you afraid?"

Simply put, past and future individual interpretations can be described through words if we but ask. And these questions are imperative if we are to understand the feelings and experiences of our adult children.

Those events that are felt as restraining forces by one person may not be felt as such by others, especially others of different generations. The Murdocks and the Holts may have understood what their children were saying or may have superimposed their own interpretations. If they know what meaning the experiences had for their grown children, they can better judge how to enhance their children's chances for psychological growth.

An in-depth search of meaning could reveal other ramifications. The Holts' son, George, called home perhaps most obviously for sheer physical help, but also because during times of loss adult children:

1. *Need to touch home base for security.* A person who is cared about wants overt demonstrations of that love. George believed his parents had a lifelong loving investment in his welfare. He needed to feel that security again, and assumed it was reasonable to touch bases when he was in danger of being thrown out while running. He can go on and leave the field once he feels safe. Someone *cares*.

2. *Need to describe each step leading to the events and feelings about it in order to deal with the grief.* Note that expression of feelings is essential and should not be discounted with an "Oh, this is the best in the long run" attitude. Active listening is required.

3. *Need to align goals and recognize worth in new experiences.* Once the feelings, love, and events

are manifest, the Holts can evoke the model of the confident, capable son they and he hold. Once a secure foundation exists, the adult child can move on to meet this need and to terminate the needed attachment to home base. If George *did* want his parents to take the children, they should ascertain the reasons and explore the alternatives. The limits of such help should be clearly and strictly spelled out.

The maturing adult's psychological growth— as well as that of the parents—can proceed when restraining forces are lessened. Each direction implies its opposite.

Since George Holt is in his late thirties, he has experienced a different time frame than have his parents. George has not experienced, for instance, a world war, but a time of comparative peace. He has probably consolidated self in work, learned to organize time, and is now learning how to focus upon problems in family intimacies.

The Murdock daughter, Carolyn, had not called her parents. Whether or not they thought they provided a caring atmosphere that freed her to explore her own inclinations, she had opted to stick to her picture of being married to a spouse who loves, respects, and notices her. While she had gone to the crisis center, she also returned to her husband and the crisis-provoking atmosphere he generated. When we stay in a *punitive situation*, we:

1. *Need to cling to secure attachment/affection.* Carolyn has not construed being beaten up as reason enough to leave. The Murdocks' role is

to try to understand her view. Does she believe
her parents will say, "I told you so?" Do she
and her husband have a genuinely loving relationship and simply need professional help in
handling frustrations? Does she not believe
her parents care for her and are able to offer
emotional support? Does a women's support
group exist for her?

2. *Need to identify rational and irrational beliefs.*
Carolyn needs to examine whether she believes she and her child deserve to be hit,
because "it's the husband's place to discipline
the family"—an irrational belief. She needs to
describe her incomplete picture of perceived
probabilities and possible consequences. How
goals and decisions are, in reality, being made,
and some revised dimension should be discussed. This rational approach is fraught with
emotion, but dissipates wishful thinking,
fears, or ignoring reality—which constitute irrational processes in the representational
model of the world she holds.

3. *Need to consider ways to eliminate the threat.*
Carolyn grew up without having to face problems of survival as well as with peer pressures
to sleep around and experiment with drugs
and with opportunities to overthrow es-
tablished ways of doing things. She responded
by opting for marriage, although in doing so
she went from one protected environment into
another. She stood up to her parents' objec-
tions to her marital choice. She *has* made
decisions as to leaving one situation for another, or trying to make situations more suit-

able to her desires. An action that would lead to continued broadening of her psychological growth would be to take a stance of "this will not be a violent family" and progress from there. Her alternative action could be leaving, finding a job and/or someone else, et cetera.

As a person grows psychologically (that is, as the spiral moves outward), his or her life space expands. The broadening experiences differ greatly among generations. The types of experiences we parents of grown children enjoyed as "broadening" are occurring at earlier and earlier ages. For example, our first plane ride was at age twenty-five, our grandparents' at age eighty, and our children's at age eight or younger. Our parents may have traveled by covered wagon, steamship, steam-engine train, propeller-driven craft, and we travel by jet. Also, we assumed more responsibility for family and personal survival in our youth than our children do today. So, what might be growth-producing for these adult children could be experience in making hard decisions, taking financial and maintenance responsibilities for their families and making do.

A person with an expanded life space has more room to draw upon, and can deal psychologically with the more distant past and with the future. The less psychological growth experienced, the less one is able to deal in those time frames. Thus, the extent of psychological growth and the size of life space reflect one another.

When parents have discussions that involve decisions by young children, they base their understanding upon limited information.

Many parents have wryly observed that their

children perceive being given "information" as being given "advice." Both advice and fear of unknown consequences cause some adolescents to become stiff-necked and stubborn and others to become indecisive. Carolyn seems caught at this wavering adolescent stage, ignoring reality. She must ask herself, "What do I fear? How and why do I fear it?"

Unknown wishes and fears can color one's view of reality—past, present and future. Carolyn fears the chance of making a decision as potentially incongruous as the original decision that united her with a seemingly loving person who turned out to be violent. She needs to ask, "What is the worst possible consequence of terminating this relationship? What is the best? What is the worst possible thing that could result from seeking help? The best?"

Perceived probabilities and possible consequences will undoubtedly clash with wishful thinking.

She also needs to examine what she believes are her strengths and weaknesses. She is an adult woman, deserving of respect, and is at the stage to examine goals. The question is, how can her parents help her to examine her present situation realistically?

During periods when *inward* forces are stronger, there is stunted psychological growth. This can occur when a "double-bind," or approach-avoidance situation is present. When the opposing forces are *equal*, a psychological growth stalemate occurs. When *outward* forces are greater, growth results.

Both Carolyn and George are caught in potential double-binds: society's view of a "good parent" who provides the best possible environment for the child, versus their own needs for emotional support.

A period of no growth can be a period of retrenchment. The individual may be so caught up in survival that no future orientation and no external events cause any impact.

People who live very routine lives and those who cannot risk change would be described by a smaller cylinder, similar to that of youngsters. Those more open to experience or those who have fewer demands placed upon them represent the opposite. Sickness, also, can contribute to periods of no growth.

The demands on the Holts' son include the logistics of arranging for child care and transportation for his children at both ends of the workday. The demands upon George prevent his giving any attention to any long-range goals: his goal is merely to get through each day. Coupled with George's unhappiness at the loss of a loved one is his need for emotional support during his attempt to gain control of the situation. Meeting his responsibilities will further reinforce a positive self-concept.

The longer a person remains at lower levels of psychological well-being, the more difficult it may be to move toward growth. A person can deal with only so much at a given time. Time itself, on the other hand, is often helpful in bringing matters under control and gaining strength to meet more difficult challenges.

Hope is also a powerful tool and one which parents can generate through verbal support of their children. It can permeate a person's life. When people experience depression or relative lows, previous learning, trial and error activities, or a supportive atmosphere are resources for the person to use while dealing with current depression.

It is important for a person to have time to recognize his or her state of mind and examine feelings.

Communication skills play an important part of the helping process between parents and children. Children—especially in their late teens and early twenties—often find it difficult, but must learn, to express their emotions to their parents. Parent and child each need to describe his or her feelings, events, problems, consequences, and possible alternative actions. *Active listening* and *feedback* are essential communication skills.

The following are some helpful guidelines to be used in communicating effectively:

ACTIVE LISTENING

1. Clarify what the person is saying.
2. Wear the other person's shoes: understand what feelings are present, and convey understanding.
3. Do not give opinions or advice while the person is explaining; the time for input will come later.
4. Do not interpret for the person; let the speaker describe his or her own perspective.

FEEDBACK

1. When giving feedback, share a statement of personal feelings first; that is, admit the observation is subjective.
2. Do not hurry to interpose a response.
3. If there are implied criticisms, also try to

include *positive* comments on the other's underlying feelings, expectations, and intents.

4. Where appropriate, conclude with a clear-cut statement of behavior one would like to see from the other person, but show empathy in doing so: "I know you have a reason to behave as you do."

Feedback involves *demonstrating love and support* by touch, word, and action so that young adults recognize their own strengths and how much their parents care for them.

The third part of the helping process is for the parents to base their understanding on *their own* similar feelings in similar situations. The content may be different in each situation, but everyone goes through similar events. Parents can relate to a loss: everyone has lost a pet, a job, a revered colleague, a close friend, a relative. Parents can relate to remaining within a punitive situation: everyone has been in a classroom where failure or denigration of self was present, in a job under a harsh boss, in a world that threatens nuclear war, or in war as a participant.

The three parts of the helping process underlie tactics addressed in subsequent chapters.

CHAPTER FOUR

MOTIVATING COMPLACENT, DEPENDENT CHILDREN

"My mother," Manuel told the other foster grandparents, "worked seventeen hours a day scrubbing floors so that I could graduate from high school. I set up my little business and worked seven days a week so that my kids wouldn't have to scrub floors or work seven days a week. I sent them all through college. Now they won't work at all. If someone looks cross-eyed at them, they quit their jobs. They are always sleeping late, slow-moving, dull and passive. They have no goals and won't move off dead center. I don't know what has become of my hopes that they would better themselves."

"Sounds like the old saying, 'Shirtsleeves to shirtsleeves in three generations,'" said a balding man across the room.

"My youngest daughter dropped out of high school," plump and graying Mrs. Williamson volunteered sadly. "I wanted her to be a nurse, but her ideas were different from mine. She has been sitting in my house for ten years now."

"The worst thing about my kids," said Mr. Ramirez, brushing his black hair back with his fingers, "is that they all think they can move back in on me anytime they want. They don't realize that they are adults who should take care of themselves."

There are a few possible causes of such immobility in young adults. One is that it's been learned. Other causes can be fear, insecurity, or physical illness. A learned pattern of behavior is self-perpetuating. And young adults who have fallen into a pattern of no growth exhibit fear, laziness, refusal to talk about the future, and dependence on others to care for them.

The children being discussed by the foster grandparents at the beginning of this chapter failed to acquire techniques of purposeful living along the way. They are missing what some theorists call a sense of *self-efficacy*, or the ability to monitor life. Their lack of motivation is due to not thinking about what goals are desirable and how one might achieve them. Because the pattern has become entrenched, these children might need professional help to change; strong inward forces have to be identified and dealt with so that psychological growth can proceed.

Certainly such dependent young adults cannot feel productive. If the problem is one of taking a look at oneself and one's future, the parent can help by providing a sounding board. Unless the young adult wants to change, however, it is difficult to proceed. But, fortunately, people do tire of being ineffective and dependent, and, when they do parents can assist them in adopting more goal-oriented actions.

Some useful strategies are needed to help adult children toward psychological growth. The helping process outlined in the last chapter should be employed along with the subsequent strategies which will be discussed.

To the parent, grown children who seem to be immobile and dependent have taken what appears to be an easy path. Someone else has the financial burden, the decisions to make, the responsibility. Yet, it's often that the dependent young person fears making decisions, and does not want to take the risks. Thus, his or her life space decreases or never expands. There is no sense of time perspective or long-range planning or commitment to a goal. The dependence may result from prior childhood learning situations—which can be replaced by new learning. It may be from emotional tensions—which can be reduced and brought under control. It may be from frustration—which involves solving the frustration or learning ways to go around it. It may be from insecurity, with any of the reasons cited above as the source—which means the person must gain confidence.

A person is motivated when there is striving to reach a goal, planning, commitment, and willingness to proceed. First, however, the person has to want the goal and sense that it is within probability to achieve.

Babies' motivations are to be cared for—to have food, dry diapers, cuddling. We see toddlers, striving to satisfy curiosity, asking questions such as: "Does God have arms? Where do measles come from? Where does the dark go? What is dirt made of?" Children are social creatures and want to do things right. As they grow older, it becomes more difficult to find the goal or end-product they think is worthy of expending energy on to achieve. This is because cognition becomes more complicated.

Because action in seeking a goal requires the expenditure of energy, the young person has to perceive some chance of success in attaining it. If the person perceives threats to his or her self-esteem, the easiest coping strategy is to not attempt action and expend the energy. The threats may consist of negative feedback in the form of ridicule, negative evaluation, or questioning the child's ability to understand directions. Whatever the reason, a mental picture has been created for the maturing child that one is safer not trying to achieve a goal than trying to achieve one that is unattainable.

Often the very terms "success" and "failure" have not been defined. The grown child has a vague idea of each concept without being able to define specifically what is meant. He or she can be helped by talking about definitions: "How will you know when you are successful? Is it a certain salary? A certain end-product? Working at one job for sixty days without trouble with the boss?"

If, however, the young adult has been prevented from reaching a goal, it is necessary to assist him or her in identifying the barriers as well as the forces that can be used to help achieve the goal. Simply identifying a problem is not enough; some solutions must also be considered.

Ordinarily, attacks on barriers can take one of three forms:

1. Go through the barrier, bowl it down, make it impotent.

2. Go around the barrier, find other paths, allow it to remain, but do not allow it to block the goal.
3. Leave the field, do not try for the goal, give up.

The unmotivated, dependent young person has left the field and quit trying, whatever the reason. Unless he or she feels that there's a valid reason to go through or around the barriers to a goal, the person will often stay in limbo, sometimes for months or even years.

Parents have goals, too. Perhaps the grown child chooses not to recognize hints about "getting through school" or "getting a job," "getting a place to live." Then parents must stop hinting and set limits. Ask about goals and plans and have an adult discussion about barriers and how you, as a parent, can help foster more appropriate action. In most cases, it is probably best to initially help them identify their personal strengths and values, the most effective uses of energy, or the ways to meet challenges. Some young adults are better approached with an ultimatum. Still others have to learn to sort out their own and parents' needs before attempting action.

As illustrated in Figure 4–1, the person who is not growing continues to have a restricted lifespace and lacks experiences necessary to be a wholly functioning individual. If the life space is small or the experiences lack depth, the individual is often subject to irrational or vague fears. "Not to decide" is a decision that may be the best tactic the young adult has been able to make.

Of course, the grown child may have a physical problem. There are several physiological causes

TABLE 4-1

PSYCHOLOGICAL GROWTH AND MOTIVATION

PSYCHOLOGICAL GROWTH	STUNTED GROWTH
Awareness of personal Characteristics	*Unaware*
Independent	Dependent
Capable	Ignores strengths
Preferences and values	Undifferentiated values
Confident	Withdrawn
Tension channeled	Tense
Expending serious effort	*Lackadaisical*
Life space expanding	No growth
Alternatives available for action	Frustrated
Problem-solving	Indecisive
Oriented to past, present, future	Ignores time
Long-range planning	No planning
Commitment to goal	Uncommitted
Meeting change willingly	*Insecure*
Decision-making	Fearful
Risk-taking	Free-floating
Commitment to self and others	*Disrespectful*
Active	Inactive
Concerned	Unconcerned

for lack of energy, and these can be treated if they're identified.

Parents who have experienced healthy psychological growth will have both broader expanses and profounder ranges to draw from than those with restricted or less enriched backgrounds (as shown in the figure). Obviously, restricted experiences furnish a smaller basis for making projections into the future. People inevitably bring past experience to bear on present situations.

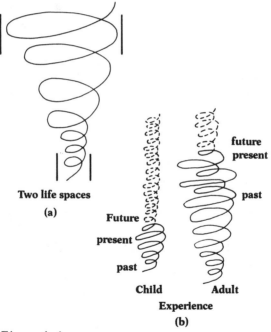

Figure 4–1
Psychological growth as viewed from a) a restricted and a growth period and b) from the past, present and future experiences that a child and adult can draw on.

Strategies for helping young adults to become conscious of their personal characteristics and for demonstrating commitment to themselves and others should be varied and fluid. Helping a young adult overcome pervasive feelings of ineptitude and dependency requires time. The person cannot be *told* to "be confident right now." If the parent can, with the child, assess past problematic situations overcome, then the grown child can begin to accept the fact that people make mistakes and that he or she is capable of caring for himself.

Parent and child can discuss directing energy toward the child's goal and toward meeting change. A helpful technique in structuring strategies is to put them down on paper. Throughout, ongoing moral support will be needed from the parent.

Be demonstrative about your love and care. Insecure young people can't guess.

Listen to your offspring. Hear the words and emotions. Comment and discuss his or her words and emotions, not your own.

Repeat the child's words. i.e. "I didn't ask to be born."

Or paraphrase his or her feelings. "You're thinking life is hard and unfair and you did not choose to have to go through it. Or maybe, you think I am being unfair and am trying to shirk my duty. What do you see as my duty to you at this stage of your life?"

Provide feedback after the young adult has had a full chance to be heard. If criticizing, also comment on the child's good intentions and positive characteristics. "I did want you to be born. I loved you and cared for you. Because I still care for you and your well-being, I am concerned about your future plans. I have a need to explore those plans with you, because right now I am hazy about what you are thinking and I would feel better if you could tell me your dreams or plans, even if they are somewhat uncertain."

Base your guidance on your experience in previous transition periods in your own life. Recall your feelings—fear, uncertainty, trepidation, adventuresomeness—and gambling decisions about the unknown. Make your own imperfections known to your children.

Go slowly. The issues between your children and you have built up over time and can be surmounted over time. As noted in the comments on strategies, some problems take a much longer time than others to solve.

Commit time. "We have to talk, you and I. Is now okay, or is seven o'clock tonight better?"

Set some new ground rules. "You have probably noticed I've felt some strain over our relationship. I need to put it into words and, if I seem unreasonable bear with me, continue the discussion, don't walk out, and I promise you the same caring treatment. I cannot continue the financial and mental strain I keep assuming for myself, because you are an adult and it is not my place to do so. I want to help you work out plans and give you moral support while you achieve them. This will probably take some hours, so let's set a schedule whereby we can abandon other commitments and set aside time for discussion."

Awareness of personal characteristics and commitment to self and others develop over time. While there seem to be more songs about love than hate and about commitment rather than unconcern, there are fewer *spoken* words. Negative comments and criti-

cisms are voiced by parents more often than is positive feedback. Thus self confidence, which is especially shaky during the late teens, can erode. We do
not capitalize on all the tensions we do handle and we
tend not to remember nor dwell on successful experiences. So at first, as parents, we can practice by
recalling our own past non-successes in order to give
advice to our children.

Try to recall all the situations in the past year
when your blood pressure rose, adrenalin flowed, jaw
clenched, back tightened up, you chewed your nails,
flared out at someone. For each incident recall how
you alleviated the tension. Did you count to ten? Did
you rearrange furniture or pull weeds? Did you take a
warm bath? Play tennis or jog? Set aside a time to
worry and make plans? Jot down all your ways of
handling frustration. Do you think this list has
changed over time?

Now you are ready to help your grown child to
recognize, bit by bit, the myriad ways of dealing with
tension and frustration. Let him or her say aloud
what a particular situation entails, but do not let the
problem stand with the reaction left unspoken. Do
the same with the next situation. Since most people
find it easy to complain and recite "downers," begin
by helping the adult child learn to describe difficult
situations so that the described reactions become
part of his or her confidence in dealing with setbacks.

A person learns to adopt new behavioral patterns when old habits fail to bring desired results. A
parent trap exists in making the decisions and doing
the chores for one's children; it often seems easier
than waiting for the expected change or living with a

mess. Better coping strategies are: demonstrate, supervise rehearsal, disappear. Put your attention elsewhere. Refuse to enforce dependency. Smile, but don't intervene.

Until people examine their successes or the myriad skills they use every day, they behave as though they "can't." Teach your growing adult self confidence.

Think of three successful experiences, beginning as early in your life as you can. Specify *how* you were successful. Tell your young adult child about it. Ask him or her to remember his or her earliest successful experience. Comment on the skills he or she showed. Introduce an observation of an experience you remember when he or she was successful. Introduce variations on this theme over a long period of time, and conclude each time with a comment on a strength the adult child has shown.

Trace through all the tasks you completed the day before, the week before, the month before. List the steps completed successfully and what skill was shown: management, organization, budgeting, task completion, consumer skills, interpersonal skills. The individual tasks can be grouped under broad categories such as these. Do not forget the interpersonal skills. Ask your young adult to compare notes in a similar time frame or help you organize the skills and then, using these as examples, have him or her draw out similar conclusions from his or her experiences. This tactic is often used to help people with no paid work experience to document what they can do that would be useful to an employer.

Commitment to self can sometimes be escalated by paying attention to larger concerns in the community or with helping in some capacity. The range of volunteer opportunities is enormous. However, unmotivated young people have to be catapulted into taking them. When you are in immediate, dire need of assistance to carry out some volunteer task, give a cry for help that demands that your young adult child help you navigate your way through the task. Expect help upon request on future such occasions. Gradually place the young person in situations requiring total responsibility for a one-shot, time-limited volunteer task; the heady experience of being needed is a powerful reward. Volunteer work is a source of skills for young people.

In trying to build up confidence by cheerful exhortation that the young adult is a "good" person, the parent risks rejection because the child was in the process of thinking "bad" thoughts. It is better to comment on particularly well done tasks; on the strengths involved in carrying out such tasks.

Expenditure of energy and acceptance of change are intertwined. In order for the grown child to stop poor reactions and meet experiences with new behavior patterns, the frustrations and fears of risk-taking must be approached. As Figure 4-2 shows, barriers have to be dealt with in order to furnish opportunities for growth. If you demonstrate that you care about the young person, such barriers to change can be challenged from the security of a safe environment, and the primary focus can be on the positive strengths shown by the child, even in his or her failure to broach the barrier.

The following suggestions can be adapted in any order so that positive changes of behaviors and reactions occur.

Daydreams. Think back to daydreams you can remember. Was there any common theme? How old were you when each one occurred? Now picture yourself ten years from today. Where are you working? What are you wearing? What setting are you in? How much do you make? What satisfactions do you get from the job? What are the dissatisfactions you have learned to live with? Who are your colleagues and your superior? Where do you live? What do you do with your leisure time? Try this analyzing activity with your adult children. Discuss both yours and your adult child's reflections.

Lifeline. Draw a line across a page. Mark each point with a major decision or major shift that occurred in your life. Put stick figures in place for people who had the most influence along the line of that event. (You may begin with birth at one end and as far in the future as you can predict at the other; or you can begin with childhood or adolescence.) Put a star for each positive occurrence. Put an unsmiling face (the opposite of the one for "Have a Happy Day") for each negative. Try this exercise with members of your family. Discuss yours and the child's memories.

Name one thing you want to do. This strategy is sometimes called force-field analysis. Draw a line from top to bottom the length of a page. At the top put something you want to do. On one side list all those "forces" that you can use to help you achieve the goal. On the other side list all the barriers. Assign points from one, for "little force," to ten, for "major force." Draw arrows between the positive forces that could help overcome the negative forces. Draw a line through those negative forces you can do nothing about. If a line is drawn though a major negative

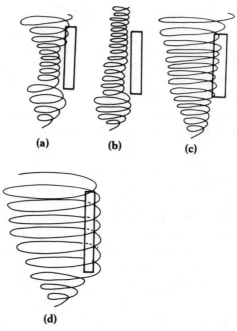

Figure 4–2
Barriers to psychological growth can affect individual spirals differently. Four people respond in differing manners in the above illustrations: a) Upon encountering the barrier, the individual withdraws until a period in time when the person feels psychologically prepared to tackle the barrier. b) Upon encountering the barrier, the individual withdraws but unfortunately is never able to grow again, even though the barrier is no longer present. c) Upon encountering the barrier, the individual is able to continue growing psychologically while dealing with the barrier. d) Upon encountering the barrier, the individual is able to grow enough psychologically to deal with the barrier.

force, turn the page over and list alternative means of going around, ignoring, or otherwise averting the danger of giving up. Try this on your young adult, using his or her future goal.

Alternatives. Don't hesitate to use a sense of humor. When you set out to generate a list of alternatives, let your mind freewheel. Using the goal designated in the previous paragraph or another goal, list all the alternatives for reaching it you can. For example, if a goal is to "send love long-distance," you might list "skywriting, Candygram, flowers, telegram, tom-toms, singing telegram, note in a bottle." Choose three actions with the most probability of your being able to achieve them. Try this exercise with the entire family.

Barrier person. If a barrier is caused by a frustrating experience with another person, make a concrete statement of the problem. Who? When? How? What? Where? Why? Identify the behavior the other person shows when the barrier is in place. Think about what you have observed about people in that position. What do they feel, specifically what emotion? How does one reduce the welling up of such an emotion? What are your alternatives? List these and assign points on the basis of feasibility: What is most likely to work will get the most points. Practice creating a situation which will use the best emotion-reducing technique. Try it out on that person. If it doesn't seem to work, try the next approach. Use this strategy to help the young adult identify, choose, and practice an approach to someone else. Let your maturing child try this strategy, but be sure that there is a commitment to discuss it with you later. If you have to fall back and regroup, do it with dignity and no recriminations.

Take one small step. Problem solving involves all of the above steps. Many small decisions have to be made in everyday life. Daydreams and goals, the direction of life, alternatives, probability, possibility, and barriers are dealt with all the time. People who are unmotivated often fear making conscious an unconscious choice, because it might be the wrong one. However, though every decision colors every later decision, directions can change.

In order to be oriented toward the future, a person must take small steps each day toward that future. Each successfully completed small step rewards the direction the person is taking. In order to help the maturing child grow, the parent often must assist him or her in starting to move toward a distant major goal—if only by focussing on an interim step.

Set down some small steps that successful adults take toward either a long-range or immediate goal, and indicate how your young adult can know the step has been completed. Discuss a "hazy" or explicit goal held by your young adult child and make a list of small steps, each of which should have an observable end. If one does not work, do not discuss excuses; together, merely restate the step.

Make sure that a schedule for discussing the step has been agreed upon beforehand, lest you be accused of "hassling." If no excuses are permitted, there are no justifications for avoiding the step. The only point to be discussed is "do you really want to achieve this goal to be in a better position?"

Successes are rewarding in themselves, but a

cheerful reaction with a hug or smile is also appropriate. A moderate state of anxiety increases performance. Too much or too little anxiety does not contribute to better performance. Young and middle-aged adults who are overcome by anxiety often lack the will to move ahead. There are many ways of reducing anxiety, depending upon the situation. Parents should try to recall how they have handled "butterflies," final exams, near misses in a car. Some tactics are: to breathe deeply, think about another subject, work hard at something else until the last minute, picture the audience in their underwear, or engage in relaxation exercises.

Not all anxiety should be reduced, however, for energy is based upon activity. After you and your child learn to define a problem clearly, to state options, and to choose one for trial, the anxiety levels should be reduced to only just beyond the point where it stops him or her from taking some course of action.

Finally, an emotional support system is needed while the maturing adult sorts out the options. The trial might not work and the temptation, for an insecure young adult, is to give up rather than risk more anxiety. A caring parent can help stop such flight and assist the young adult in re-thinking the problem, alternatives, and decisions.

CHAPTER FIVE

DEALING WITH YOUNG ADULTS' DEPRESSION

"Mealy-mouthed. That's what he is. Always whining about something," brusque, red-haired Mrs. Lefebre complained. "My middle son is never happy with anything. He is always down in the dumps. I keep telling him to cheer up, but to no avail."

"My dad once told me," injected motherly Mrs. Blesty, "about a fellow whose father said, 'Cheer up, things could be worse.' So he did cheer up, and things *did* get worse!"

Mrs. Lefebre blinked. "I'm serious. He is so blue all the time that it casts a pall over every family gathering. I am worried about him. He finds no joy in life. Every day is Black Friday. I don't know how to talk to him anymore."

Many young adults are faced with disillusionment over their powerlessness. Changing, chaotic world conditions lead them to believe that no one is interested in their dreams for the future. Moreover, the child-centered environment in which many of them spent their early years has convinced them that the world would always be loving toward them and devoted to their well being. The realization that each has to make his or her lonely way in this world, facing Goliaths of indifference, is a rude awakening.

Young adults often have not discovered the right combination of behaviors that are the keys to bringing their world under control. They do not know how to go about filling their lives with caring people, developing relationships and finding fulfilling work. They have no equipment with which to make their ways. So they give up when the road becomes rocky.

It must be realized that the moment-to-moment forces which positively or negatively influence a person's psychological growth spiral—the curve of life experiences—are far from smooth, as shown in Figure 5–1(a). If life were smooth, the figure would be flat, like that in 5-1(b).

In reality, the development of the individual *is* irregular. The uneven nature of psychological growth is reflected in the changes of life space.

Many young adults have little knowledge of life's very real impediments; they expect a smooth spiral and are more than likely to get a rough one. The irregular nature of psychological spirals accounts for the frequent depressions or "blues" experienced by some young people.

When young adults are in deep depression or a life-threatening mood, they should be referred for professional help immediately. Any family-member support during such a stressful period is also extremely important.

The young adult who usually functions at

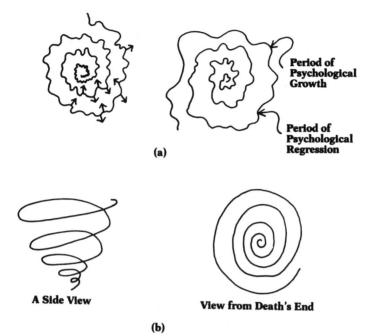

(a)

Period of
Psychological
Growth

Period of
Psychological
Regression

A Side View   View from Death's End

(b)

Figure 5–1
*(a) Segment of a psychological growth spiral from the death
end showing the irregular nature, forces at work, and periods
of growth and regression, and (b) a smooth spiral illustrating
an unrealistic view of psychological development.*

higher levels of psychological growth and experiences
only an occasional low, can frequently be helped by
sincere caring concern.

As Figure 5–2 illustrates, this may be a typical
or an atypical pattern. One person may show a per-
sistent tendency to moodiness. Another may suddenly change his or her behavior in the life space,
either temporarily or permanently. This could be a
reaction to emotional tension, frustration, or a history of frustration, sickness, or insecurity.

However, if an adult child shows a decreased ability to deal with the passage of time, seems disorganized, exhibits behavior typical of much younger children, or makes threats of self-destruction, professional help is needed.

Cases of depression that have a self-destructive element may include not only threats of suicide, but also such manifestations as overeating, drugs, excessive drinking, overwork, reckless ventures such as fast driving or taking other risks with one's health and safety. Depressed people find their situations intolerable, although the same conditions would seem no more than routine to other people.

Any unusual change in life-style should be treated seriously. Some signals of serious depressions are: giving away possessions, cutting off contact with friends and relations, extreme lethargy, strange sleeping and eating habits. Get professional assistance.

If a young person has the blues, is whiney, sour, glum, or sad, parents might try a few of the growth strategies to be discussed in this chapter. Such strategies often produce good results when young people are moody but not, however, severely depressed.

It is important to note that the longer a young person remains at lower levels of psychological well-being, the more difficult it may be to move toward growth. All normal people experience depressed states or relative lows. The important thing is to do what you can to ensure that that state in your young adult children will be short-lived.

Depression will be shortest for people who, through experience or trial and error, have learned to

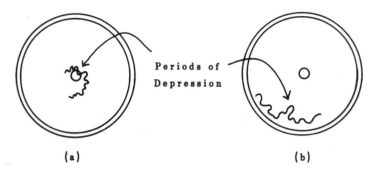

Figure 5–2
(a) A portion of a spiral showing psychological regression requiring hospitalization, and (b) showing psychological regression not requiring hospitalization.

move ahead with the business of living. For those who have failed to acquire the mechanics of countering lows, the state will be more prolonged.

Usually, time will be all a person needs to overcome a low state. However, if there does not seem to be recovery within a reasonable time span, the parent should use the active-listening technique to try to discover the reason for the low feeling. If it is a problem, the solving strategies mentioned in Chapter Four will be useful.

If the person feels impotent, then perhaps assertiveness training and changes in self-beliefs are indicated.

If the young person feels no one cares, and is not responsive to parental love and concern, then encouraging development of new interpersonal relationships is indicated.

Perhaps the young adult needs to develop some new interests and skills to overcome his or her feeling of insecurity.

If the problem is physical, a physician should monitor prescriptive measures. These could include guidance in nutrition, diet, and exercise.

A maturing adult who feels impotent because of an inability to act upon the environment can be helped by rehearsing more assertive behavior. Depending upon the person's age and life situation, a discussion of school problems, a change of jobs, or of reactions, or speaking up about an overload of tasks is often necessary for psychological well-being; the risk is obvious.

ASSERTIVENESS

Being assertive simply means being aware of the entitlement to one's rights being recognized and respected. It is not being aggressive or hostile. Assertiveness is demonstrated both in verbal and physical reactions.

A person asserting positive nonverbal behavior appears confident and forthright: direct eye contact, steady stance, firm handshake—all indications to others that a person has a good self-concept. How often do we know something is wrong when a person's shoulders slump and there is no eye-to-eye contact? Some people deliberately droop so that others will take pity, ask what is wrong, and try to right it. That kind of manipulation seldom works. People have to be up front about changes they seek.

Another poor non-verbal strategy young adults often employ is smiling when the topic is serious. They think giggling or a nervous smile reduces the "threat" to someone else. Mature adults usually do not use such plaintive tactics; they do not have to be protected. Through rehearsal, strong non-verbal aspects can become part of a person's repertoire.

Verbal behavior includes the message of the comment, and the tone in which it's delivered. Sometimes people reduce what would be an effectively assertive statement by turning it into a question: "I don't want to do that?" The little lift of the tone of voice at the end of that comment seems to indicate antagonism or derisiveness. An even tone without threat or hostility is a much better strategy.

Parents can make up a series of examples to help grown children understand the differences among being assertive, nonassertive, or aggressive. Here are some examples:

"You kids have your beds made before eight o'clock or I'll campus you for life."

"I want you children to have your beds made by eight o'clock, because we deserve to live in an orderly house. It makes us feel better."

"Would—uh—you kids—uh—make your beds, tomorrow, *please?*"

The first statement is aggressive—in words as well as tone of voice. The second is assertive. The third is non-assertive—and equally as ineffective—as the aggressive statement.

We can all think of numerous examples of questions that by wording and tone of voice demonstrate these various approaches. Those that might be thought of as appropriate to the impotent young person's situation can be rehearsed.

Three more examples of such statements are:

"I cannot work late tonight to finish this letter you just handed me, but I'll be happy to do it first thing tomorrow, or you can ask someone else to do it."

"I—uh—okay."

"I don't get any damn overtime for doing stuff you drop on my desk at the last minute."

"Polishing this last piece is not part of my job, but I am complimented you asked me, and I will be happy to teach Jake exactly what you want."

"That's not my job and I resent it when you expect to manipulate me by phony compliments."

"Well, if I have to . . ."

"That's a piece of junk!"

"Okay, I'll take it but it's not exactly . . ."

"I don't think that is very well made, and it is not what I had in mind. I'll look elsewhere, thank you."

These examples are what we call "protective assertions." They give a person the option of asserting his or her own rights without stepping on someone else's toes or running roughshod over another person.

There is another class of assertions that is different from those that teach a person how to say "no." This deals with being assertive in social gatherings, known as personal or social assertiveness.

Many young adults have trouble meeting people in new situations. Personal or social assertions teach them how to make small talk and new friends. Small talk can grow out of engaging oneself in active listening to another person's experiences or from sharing a similar experience, without playing "can you top this?"

Three examples of using young peoples' experiences in helping them choose appropriate behavior strategies are:

"I, too, found the Spanish people dignified and warm. I really enjoyed that part of my trip, as you did."

"Oh, that's nice."

"Well, when I went to Europe I came back convinced that America is the only place, and anyone who thinks differently is crazy."

Three more might be:

"I don't do anything interesting."

"I read the best book last night. It confirmed my belief that free enterprise is the American way of life and there is *no* other way."

"I read an interesting book about free enterprise. What do you think of the premise that capitalism is alive and well?"

Part of personal or social skills is learning to give and receive compliments. Receiving compliments is not easy, and young people can be helped to perceive effects through examples such as:

"What, this old dress?" (insults the speaker).

"Thank you. I'm glad you like it, too." (compliments the speaker)

"Oh—uh—well . . ." (does not give the speaker feedback)

Other good examples are:

"I am glad you enjoyed my performance. Thank you." (positive response)

"Oh no, I botched up the second act terribly, and my dress tore on the set! It was a disaster!" (negative response)

"Do you really think I did okay?'' (noncommunicative response)

Giving effective compliments is difficult for some young people. Illustrative examples of this skill are helpful:

"Your report was very well done. I could easily follow how one could move from beginning to conclusions."

"Nice seeing you again."

"Well, I guess it was pretty hard standing up in front of all those people and trying to communicate."

"That was a most enjoyable evening because you were so thoughtful and charming."

"See you later."

"Well, even if I do say so myself, this has been

a great evening. I had a magnificent steak and all I could drink."

Practicing ways to say "no," giving and receiving compliments, and making small talk helps the non-assertive young person who otherwise feels somewhat victimized by other—often older, more authoritarian—people.

The third part of assertiveness rehearsal has to do with the person's belief system. As mentioned earlier, young adults tend to feel they should do everything right, know everything about new situations, and always put other people first. In fact, people have a right to make mistakes and to acknowledge those as a way of learning how to do things right. They have a right to ask questions. They have a right to have their own needs met.

The rational person knows that everyone has rights. Sometimes it is quite acceptable to allow someone else's needs to be met, but that should be a choice. Other situations dictate one's own needs to be paramount, and are also a correct choice.

People have a right to know the circumstances under which they must perform. They have a right to anticipate limits upon others' expectations of them. They have a right to expect other people to do their share and not exploit situations.

People have a right to expect performance from what they buy. And on the other side of the coin, manufacturers have a right not to have ill-used products returned to them as faulty.

People have a right to set their own goals and work toward them. They have a right to expect support, as well as to give it.

The assertive person's belief system will be

that of a confident, courageous human being who will not be used without choosing to be.

TEACHING SOCIAL BEHAVIOR

With the proper belief in oneself as a dignified human being, the cultivation of inner potential can proceed. And with assertive personal or social skills rehearsed and ready to be tested in the social environment, young adults can begin to risk new relationships or resolve conflicts in existing ones. Sometimes interpersonal conflicts can be handled through the problem-solving techniques mentioned in Chapter Four. That is, the problem can be clearly identified, possible solutions discussed, a choice made and tested, the choice evaluated for its usefulness or discarded and, if necessary, an alternative chosen.

Otherwise, intelligent but inexperienced adults may miss cues as to proper behavior. Behavior is usually a reaction to cues in the environment, in the situation, or from other people. So, a person who laughs at the wrong time, or makes a serious comment and becomes angry when others are kidding, or interrupts or dominates conversation will not be socially successful.

When cues to proper behavior are missed, the socially inept young adult may feel confused and slightly embarrassed without knowing why, and this can lead to guilt and self-flagellation. When such feelings are obvious, a teachable moment has arrived. One approach is to suggest that your adult child observe or recall how the best model of how one would wish to be seen behaves. Identifying the person's exact verbal and non-verbal behaviors, and then imitating them, gives young people visual feedback which will show where he or she may have made mistakes.

If the young adult cannot identify an adult to emulate, then gentle suggestions may be offered along with evidence of loving concern. This may be a hug, a smile, or a simple statement. At first rehearsal should take the form of role playing. And beginning role playing with an exaggerated, perhaps humorous, depiction of the inept behavior can relieve tension, as long as the portrayal is not sardonic. The next rehearsal should be in an easily controlled situation, in order to ensure some success. Then the positive experience should be discussed. Experience with feedback is the best experience.

Young adults will probably have to be taught how to listen or to watch other people's non-verbal cues: the tone of voice, the hands, the eyes, and the stance. They may need to learn to *hear* what other people are saying. Try saying, "I don't want any," alternating the accent on each separate word. Then ask the young adult exactly what you are trying to convey.

If the young adult is entering a new school or beginning a new job and seems perplexed by an authority figure, ask him or her to describe in detail a particular incident that was puzzling. Help identify the reaction of the third party to what was said and done. Then work on helping him or her identify alternative ways of handling the situation in order to get other reactions.

There are appropriate times to ask questions. There are times to socialize. There are appropriate behaviors, such as sitting in chairs versus upon desks, talking or making phone calls during breaks versus during work or class hours, smoking in designated areas versus in elevators where it is not permitted. Finally, the cues that young adults should pick up are exemplified in the active listening and feedback strategies described in Chapter Three. They can learn and practice active listening.

Changing their daily routine can help young adults through low periods. The change should include a new interest.

Doing even one small thing differently can be beneficial. This could be setting aside time to attend some free regular community offering. Going to church, synagogue, or temple for several weeks might lead to joining in with a study, social, or service group. Taking lessons in cookery, sewing, pottery, or golf might lead to small groups of new friends who do round-robin activities at each others' homes. A class or reading group, duplicate bridge or a local art exhibit could lead to a new interest.

The best procedure is to set a goal of one small step at a time. If other things develop, fine. Consider them unexpected benefits. But for most insecure young adults, that first step is risky enough. The possible advantages of a greater undertaking need not be voiced. Engaging the first step is reward and goal enough.

CHAPTER SIX

DEALING WITH PHYSICAL AND BEHAVIORAL ADDICTIONS

"I walked into my kids' room and found the strangest looking bottle with rubbery tubes sticking out of the top. It was some kind of drug paraphernalia. I was shocked! I thought that after seeing what alcohol did to their father they would swear off any kind of addiction," said haggard-looking Nancy O'Donnell. "I'm concerned that they'll ruin their minds and eventually their lives. How will they ever be able to be responsible parents?"

"My son hasn't turned to drugs, but we think that he's an alcoholic. If he's not going for beers with his friends and staying out most of the night, then he's sitting at home in front of the TV drinking more beer," said balding and usually jovial Mr. Jackson.

"It seems strange to me that our son, Bill, has never touched a drop of alcohol—let alone drugs—but his wife feels deserted. She says that our son doesn't spend enough time with her or his children. All he cares about is work. In fact, the school psychologist suggested that some of our grandson's hostile behavior might stem from a lack of parent-child interaction. Bill has always been such a hard working young man that we didn't ever think that any of his children would turn out anything but fine," sighed plump and gray-haired Mrs. Williams.

PHYSICAL ADDICTION

One of the more treacherous legacies of the last two decades has been the proliferation of addictions to injurious substances. Many physicians, businessmen, housewives, hippies, "good kids," and society's alienated young adults have succumbed.

The availability of an easy way to reduce stress—that of using chemical means as opposed to the conscious seeking of solutions—has touched, indeed nearly destroyed, millions of young adults. With so much drug prevalence in our society, it's incumbent upon parents to be alert to substance abuse in our young adult children.

There are three basic signals of a drug abuse problem:

(a) Physical changes in self and environment. Upon entering your young adult's room, home or apartment do you smell an unusual odor? Does your mature child's breath smell of alcohol? Do his or her clothes have a strange odor? Are his or her eyes red most of the time? Does the child act giddy or even high? Does the child "suddenly" have unexplained health problems such as loss of weight, hacking cough or nasal allergy?

(b) Changes in behavior.
As the parent keys in on the above physical changes, one should search for behavioral changes. Upon closer examination of your maturing adult's behavior do you notice that the usual early riser has become lethargic, sleeping until noon? Or when you eat with your adult child, do you find that his or her once-voracious eating habits have given way to a listless, rearrange-the-food-on-the-plate syndrome? Has your child lost interest in things which were once important (sports, studies, hobbies)? Has the young adult who a few months ago enjoyed revealing every interesting detail of the day's events suddenly become antagonized by your every question, secretive of his or her whereabouts, and defensive toward all inquiries, no matter how sincere or innocent they seem to you?

(c) Changes in personality.
Are your son's or daughter's mood swings becoming more abrupt and intense? Does he or she seem depressed or withdrawn? Has your child's personality changed? His or her response to siblings, friends or relatives?

Answers to steps above may have led you to the unfortunate conclusion that your grown child has a drug or alcohol problem.

And as all the pieces start fitting together, the picture that develops may evoke a wide spectrum of emotional reactions by the parent:

1. *Resentment and anger.* Directed at the young adult child for forcing such a problem upon the family.
2. *Guilt versus betrayal.* A conflicting combination of feelings. "Where did we fail our child? Is it our fault?" or "How could he disappoint and embarrass us this way? We've done everything for him . . . How could he *do* this?"
3. *Fear.* "What's happening and why? How are we going to handle this? We've never been through something like this; should we seek professional help?"

Now what do you do?

Any or all of the above reactions are normal and to be expected. However, once these parental adult feelings have been expressed and resolved, you must, working with the entire family, begin seeking solutions, no matter how betrayed, angry, or scared you may feel. No psychologist knows your grown child as you do. You and your spouse were *the* most important figures in your young child's life and, now again, you must become even more important if you want to save him or her.

Keep your emotions and gut reactions in hand. Your energies must be channelled toward helping your adult child through this crisis. Open up the lines of communication within the family—particularly between you and this child. After all, your adult child needs loving, caring, understanding, and direction just as much as, if not more than, when he or she was an infant. Remember, though, that the firm disciplinary hand of experience along with the nurturing will help your child gain control of the situation and resolve the problem of his or her addiction.

Replace angry, negative feelings with meaningful, positive communication. Once that takes place, your addicted young adult may begin to listen and even learn from your experience, knowledge, and strength. A foundation of honesty and support can enable your son or daughter to get professional help, enroll in a program, or accept residential care and leave drugs or alcohol behind and deal head-on with life and its problems.

Keep in mind that the family structure of today differs greatly from that of years ago. Substance problems touch step-parent families, single-parent families and natural-parent families. But whatever the configuration or composition of the family, complete and sincere communication should be attempted and, it is hoped, achieved by all. It is not helpful for either you or your grown child to ignore a substance-abuse problem. React, get involved, and try your best to get your adult child to admit his or her problem and to get help. Find out the name of an agency or counselor on drug abuse. Discuss treatment programs. Resignation will destroy your child and family much more rapidly than will his or her accusations of your meddling and interfering.

Use this unfortunate incident and take advantage of its inherent weaknesses. Build it into an opportunity to reassess with your adult child his other values, beliefs, and goals. This can be part of the therapeutic process of rebuilding your adult child's positive self-concept, one upon which to build future psychological well-being. Show your grown child what family love can accomplish.

You may lose your child for a short time through anger and resentment toward your interfering. But if you are successful, all those volatile drug- or alcohol-tainted emotions will pass, and your grown child will come to realize your love and your support—along with your determination. Such strengths will help him or her through a most dangerous period and also to repair the psychological damage that drug abuse has caused.

BEHAVIORAL ADDICTION

In order to better understand why young adults seem to suffer addictions more today than you, their parents, did as grown children, follow the conceptualizations and diagrams we use to explain this phenomenon.

Psychologist Abraham Maslow has conceptualized a hierarchy of needs which human beings attempt to meet. These needs adapt well to the spiral concept of psychological growth, as shown in Figure 6–1. The innermost, and most basic, needs must be met first. This requires comparatively less psychological growth than do more outer needs. In fact, the innermost needs are increasingly being met by society and require less effort for the individual than in previous generations.

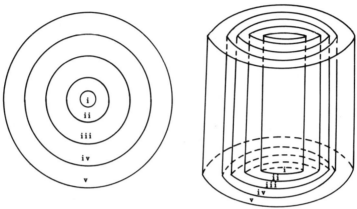

Figure 6–1
Maslow's Hierarchy of Needs adapted to the spiral concept of psychological growth. Beginning with the most basic needs they are: (i) physiological, (ii) safety and security, (iii) love and belongingness, (iv) self esteem and esteem by others, and (v) growth needs.

Previous generations, particularly those who lived through the Depression of the 1930s, were primarily forced to focus on the most basic needs: physiological and safety and security. However, our present society, through such programs as unemployment insurance, mother's allowance, and subsidized housing, has satisfied these two basic need levels. This has almost forced individuals to consider dealing with the next two levels, love and belongingness, and self esteem and esteem by others. The attainment of these is comparatively difficult, as they are as individualized as each person. And this is due to the lack of role models from previous generations. The parents, grandparents, aunts and uncles of these earlier generations were forced, by the state of the economy, to deal primarily with basic survival. The increased psychological growth required to meet "love and belongingness" tends to present more emotional pain than does fulfillment of the two lower-level needs.

Because each individual grows in his or her own manner, two people may attain very similar levels of psychological growth through very different life experiences, as represented by the paths in Figure 6–2. The psychological spirals vary, not only in the number of coils representing life experiences, but also in the length of time represented by the vertical distance.

Those individuals who move most rapidly toward meeting higher needs most often do so because they have received support and assistance during this growth process. Homes, families, or societies which relieve individuals of the task of meeting low-level needs, such as safety and security, provide a greater opportunity for the person to focus on higher-level needs and consequently, greater psychological growth.

For parents of today's adult children, this issue of satisfying different levels of basic needs may seem like mental gymnastics performed by psychologists in order to justify a job. From their perspective, Maslow's theory may not appear to have an impact upon their lives. For many married couples growing up in earlier generations, Maslow's ideas would not have appeared to be extremely relevant. Their focus was on finding a job, buying a home, and providing for their children. Compared to the present generation, little energy was utilized in pursuing education or self fulfillment, let alone self-actualization.

Now grown children are not only faced with

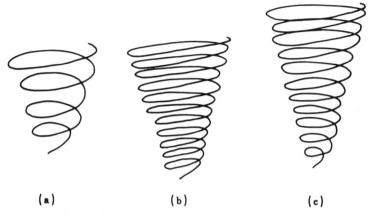

(a)   (b)   (c)

Figure 6–2
Three possible psychological spirals. All three have attained approximately the same degree of psychological growth as measured by the width of the spiral at the tops. But, (A) has fewer coils, indicating that this person has had fewer life experiences to reach this degree of psychological growth. The greater number of coils in (B) indicate more experiences in life. Finally, the growth represented by spiral (C) indicates that the same degree of psychological growth has been attained but over a longer time frame, as indicated by vertical distance.

decisions about where and how to meet basic needs but, more importantly for their parents, these young adults face increased conflict with regard to what their basic needs are—both personally and within a society which no longer provides clear paths for their lives to follow. Today's males, socialized as bread winners, are marrying more career-oriented women who want to increase their self esteem and sense of personal fulfillment. Often these women want the companionship of a male who will pursue these needs with her. Not having been adequately prepared for such a task, the couple may turn to the parents or a marriage counselor for help. The parents, or whoever begins to assume the helper role, should become familiar with what expectations their grown children have from their lives. This may be accomplished through active listening or by simply observing their lives.

However, some individuals who receive assistance or support find it virtually impossible to meet the challenges of personal growth. Some are frustrated in their attempts to grow and choose not to change their lives. This may result in a permanent setback, while for others it is temporary. Some life experiences, such as attempts to break a substance-abuse habit, may result in outward-growth pulls on their psychological spirals.

Other experiences limit psychological fulfillment and restrict the meeting of higher-level needs. Ironically, similar experiences affect people differently. One person may view himself as successful by earning twenty thousand dollars a year and owning a two-bedroom bungalow, while another with similar attainments may feel a sense of failure for not earning fifty thousand dollars a year nor owning a spacious home. The fact that people have their own individualized view of the world is a key fact parents must realize while attempting to help a grown child or further the development of a relationship.

Addictions, specifically, negative addictions, are among the psychologically limiting forces. William Glasser, author of *Positive Addiction*, has distinguished between two types of addictions: positive and negative. The former could be thought of as being an outward force upon the psychological spiral, which promotes growth. This growth, in turn, enables the individual to meet the higher-level needs described by Maslow. Similarly, negative addictions act as inward forces, restricting psychological growth and inhibiting an individual from attaining higher-order needs.

Glasser groups a wide array of substances and behaviors under the definition of negative addictions. The most common are alcohol, cocaine, and heroin; he also includes overeating and gambling as well as nicotine and caffeine.

Discovering an often-overlooked but common addiction is most often the simplest, while at the same time the most valuable step, in helping to counsel grown children. But admitting that an addiction exists is a considerably more difficult task for the grown child. There is often little acknowledgment that any kind of problem exists until much pain is experienced by the addict (and those around him or her). Significant others—spouse, parents, or friends—are often the first to realize the existence of a problem. However, it may be difficult even for parents to admit a grown child's addiction, particularly if it is non-drug-related.

Non-drug-related addictions, such as eating, gambling, or workaholism, may have been learned during youth, while the individual was very much involved in the family structure. Such an addiction may be a slight exaggeration of the behaviors exhibited by the parents or siblings. For example, parents who are thirty pounds overweight may find it difficult to confront a grown child who is eighty pounds overweight. But acknowledging that grown children have a habit which is interfering with their meeting life responsibilities need not be interpreted as a weakness of parenting skills.

Parents generally do the best job they can, given their own limitations at a particular time. It is all too easy and unproductive for parents to wallow in guilt. The first step for parents to take is to become aware and willing to acknowledge that an addiction exists. Most non-drug-related addictions share certain characteristics.

Rituals often begin as routines or habits. Carried to an extreme, they begin to interfere with life responsibilities. At that point a ritual may be reclassified as a negative addiction. Often, this behavior, when originally begun and practiced in moderation, was not only accepted but also encouraged by society. But those people who initially may have found the habit praiseworthy and may have positively reinforced the behavior, later become the very ones who object to the addiction and its negative aspects.

The fact that parents once encouraged a particular behavior often interferes with their willingness to acknowledge that circumstances change and the habit must be re-evaluated.

For example, as a young father and husband, Bill Williams assumed the responsibility to work hard to provide for his family. His wife reinforced his efforts and his parents helped him find a part-time job in the evenings to supplement his beginning wages.

Ten years later, with both Williams children in school and their mother working part-time, Bill Williams still held down his evening job. His wife insisted that he no longer needed to work; her income was more than enough to meet the material extras they enjoyed. Their ten-year-old son was exhibiting several acting-out behaviors both at home and at school. After a referral by the school principal, the school psychologist had suggested that increased parent-child contact might ameliorate many of the child's problem behaviors. What began as an understandable, if not necessary, time-consuming effort had become a negative addiction.

Bill was caught up in a routine, a ritual, which had become a way of life. The people with whom he worked part-time formed an integral part of his emotional and interpersonal support network. He felt that quitting this part-time job would change—if not end—this aspect of his life. Furthermore, he would have to fill the void of several hours each evening. Quite possibly, he would have to begin to interact with his wife and children on a level for which he was not prepared and from which he had always been excused because he was tired from working two jobs.

In the past his psychological growth had been restricted because of economic circumstances. Hanging onto the ritual of extra work, although initially done out of necessity, had sheltered Bill from meeting the psychological adjustments and subsequent growth required by life changes. Work had become a "drug" which Bill used to escape from facing further changes and challenges in life. The difficulty of Bill's situation was complicated by society's having initially encouraged his work ethic, and having continued to do so to a certain extent by labelling him "a hard worker" and "a good provider." No one had told him that the rules and requirements might change along the way.

Bill is not alone. Numerous young men and

women have been caught up in routines which served a valid purpose at one stage in life but evolved into negative addictions during a later stage. Our society is saturated with such examples.

• The young man who, as an adolescent, began tinkering with automobiles and failed to grow beyond the "auto stage" of life. As an adult he still spends most of his spare time under the hood.

• The young couple who became avid golfers as newlyweds and failed to modify their patterns when children arrived on the scene.

• The person who, as a youth, spent a great deal of time fishing and continues to spend an inordinate amount of time fishing as an adult, not realizing that this activity limits his interaction with his young children.

• The overweight teenager who has continued the poor eating habits formed during childhood and continues such patterns despite the fact that many activities are limited by poor physical conditioning.

With the changing roles of men and women and the economic necessity for both halves of a couple to work, many psychological readjustments have been required on both sexes. Parents of maturing adults sometimes need to re-evaluate their son's, daughter's, daughter-in-law's, or son-in-law's work and home roles. This may prove a difficult job for the parents, as it implies that the modelling of past generations may well be inappropriate for the today's males and females. Older people may well have been successful and fulfilled the expectations of their time, whereas for better or worse, expectations for the young adult have changed. Parents may have to seek the help of professionals or peers and friends in working with and encouraging grown children to consider altering their life styles. As parents, modelling appropriate changes may prove to be one of the most valuable methods of demonstrating that change is possible. If a child sees that others are able to acknowledge that a need to change exists and, furthermore, are willing to act on it, then he or she may be more willing to attempt self-modification. It is during these periods when the ability to listen and reflect may prove most valuable.

Behaviors which proved popular during a certain period in one's life are closely aligned to the rituals which initially may have been encouraged by society. One such example of an addiction which is popular but disruptive of family life is the "going for a drink after work" syndrome. Such behavior may have been acceptable while single but, with family responsibilities, may become a source of conflict. Some of these popular habits are justified with the line, "a person needs time to unwind." Furthermore, peer support may make any criticism of the addiction seem like nagging. In the case of some young adults, especially men, any attempt to break away from the group is not welcomed. Peers will often label a man who tries to do so "hen-pecked" in an effort to retain his membership in the group. Adult peer groups—like their adolescent counterparts—can exert strong influence in resisting change.

One way for the parents to increase awareness

of some popular addictions is to pay close attention to the media. For instance, the themes of popular music can have negative effects. One example of addiction is the teenager's over-reliance on the effects of "heavy metal" music or music whose lyrics are violent or self-destructive. Beer commercials have reinforced boys getting together for drinks with such slogans as "For all you guys out there who have worked hard all day, this [one's] for you." However, alcohol and music lyrics are not the only foci of advertising. Many individuals become clothing- or car-poor trying to stay in style with what is considered popular. Clothing and autos may not seem like negative addictions, but when such purchases begin to interfere with the fulfillment of other responsibilities, they may well be put in the category of negative addictions.

For parents, the obvious goal is to help young adults break such a cycle of self-defeating behavior. This may involve open communication with older children or direct intervention with postadolescents. Scheduling family activities directly after school or work may provide the maturing adult with an acceptable excuse to alter the pattern, and also provide a positive activity to replace the negative addiction. Providing a positive replacement activity is fundamental in establishing any new behavior patterns. Many parents are only too familiar with children who, in altering negative behavior patterns, move from one negative addiction to another. A typical example of negative replacement is the individual who quits smoking but replaces the habit with food, then gains undesired weight.

Just as habits may initially seem to be acceptable but in the end prove unacceptable, so may replacements. The current running and jogging boom provides an excellent case in point. Many people with negative addictions, such as alcoholism or overeating, have taken to the roads on foot. When done in moderation, jogging can be a positive replacement behavior. However, many young (and older) adults become involved in extreme self-imposed training programs—running, working out in gyms or on racquet and tennis courts—instead of seeking a balance between recreation and other responsibilities. Although some replacements may prove to have both positive and negative aspects, it may well be argued that at least recreational activities, whether a positive or negative addiction, are less destructive than addictions such as alcohol. In any case, friends and parents should continue to provide support and encouragement for the psychological growth necessary to leave addictive patterns behind and tackle new, more creative, behaviors.

Keeping in mind that there is usually no single source of discomfort or pain, the focus should not be solely upon the person in pain, but also on the system. Other influencing factors on the young adult's life should also be evaluated. A few of the most common are:

Work: A job which is exerting unreasonable demands or for which the individual may have set too high standards for "success."

Studies: Overly-pressured students often find their work unproductive.

Family: May be either actually imposing unreasonable expectations, or the addict may have misinterpreted what was viewed as the family's expectations.

Lifestyle: May be pushing the individual along in the "fast lane," attempting to maintain material standards which are too demanding.

As mentioned, while those most closely associated with an addict often recognize and acknowledge the existence of a problem, the young person involved may be unwilling to admit to addiction and may resist any form of help. The addiction may be a coping device to deal with the stress of feeling inadequate as a person. Although a low self esteem may not seem like a negative addiction, any habit, physical or mental, which interferes with a person's meeting life's responsibilities meets the criteria of a negative addiction. A lack of self confidence may manifest itself as a dissatisfaction with many aspects of life.

A maturing individual who moves from an addiction to negative replacement may be reflecting a negative self-concept. The roots of the addiction may date back to early childhood. Parents may recall that their young adult's typical behavior as a child was a low tolerance to frustration or a continuous striving for acceptance or recognition from others.

These underlying inferior beliefs about self may have remained unchanged in the young adult. It may be difficult for some parents to understand that a grown child who appears to be successful in many aspects of life may still view himself or herself netatively. For the individual expressing dissatisfaction with many aspects of life, the underlying issue may be a basic lack of self confidence. A husband may claim that his wife's addiction to food and the resulting weight gain is the reason for their poor marital relationship. He may, in fact, be using her weight as a cover-up for his own poor self-concept and dissatisfaction with his own life. So when his wife loses the excess weight, the relationship still may not improve, because her more attractive figure may then threaten his basic insecurity relating to his own poor self-concept.

A parent complains that her teenaged child is an alcoholic. For whatever reasons, the child does drink in excess. However, the parent focuses on the child's excesses while ignoring her own part in contributing to the situation. The parents drink in front of the teenager, rationalizing that their drinking is not part of "his problem." Neither has the strength or self confidence necessary to assume responsibility for effecting behavioral changes in their son. The underlying reason for their substance abuse may be buried deep in the complexities of their relationship. If one does not see his or her behavior objectively, it is often difficult to help oneself, let alone others. As long as the focus is on someone else, one's contributing share will not have to be dealt with.

Parents should realize that grown children may resist re-evaluating their lives for a wide variety of reasons. One may be that any change in lifestyle could be interpreted as a failure to have attained the young adult's expectations, which could have been unrealistically self-imposed or dictated by family or society, including the media's view of what successful people do and materially possess.

The demands to meet a wide range of societal expectations often generates considerable stress, and the reaction to these stresses varies from individual to individual. For some, the initial reaction may be displayed through increased irritability. Sleep patterns become irregular and disturbed in others. In an effort to alleviate the stresses, whether they be related to work, family, or economics, the individual often turns to a form of negative addiction. Alcohol or drugs have the effect of at least temporarily numbing one to the pain of the situation. Rather than allow one's self the opportunity to re-evaluate one's life to determine the source of the pain, one uses drugs as a coping device. The use of such addictions allows the mind and body a respite—a time to let the senses relax and not have to deal with the source of the discomfort. However, the real source of unhappiness continues and often the need for opiates increases.

The frustrations of living with someone who has a negative addiction but is unwilling to deal with it has led Alcoholics Anonymous to form support groups for teenagers and other family members of alcoholics. If a grown child is an addict and unwilling to admit to the problem, the family members may need to seek assistance through support groups designed to provide understanding and coping mechanisms.

CHAPTER SEVEN

THE GROWN CHILD'S SPIRITUAL WELL-BEING

"The struggles I have with my Billy and Susie all center around the strange interpretations of religion they are teaching their children," commented Mr. LaSalle, pulling the *Wall Street Journal* closer and scanning the headlines.

"My son Robby has joined a group which gathers together twice a week for meditation. They chant and teach non-violent civil disobedience. What has happened to the old-time religion we learned about?" Mrs. Reese shook her head sadly.

During the last two decades, seeking spiritual well-being has been a struggle between the modern and the traditional approaches. Television has brought the sufferings of the world into our living rooms. Minority groups, such as the physically disabled, women, and refugees, have demanded equal opportunity based on skill and ability, not random attributes of birth. Compassion for one's fellow man is a hallmark of the self-actualizing person. And churches, synagogues, and temples are being challenged to respond to current issues. The individual's relationship with God has broadened beyond finding solace in religion during periods of difficulty.

Young adults now talk of "natural highs" that come from experiences and not from the artificial means the generation of the sixties and seventies used. These "escapistic," "mind-expanding" and "consciousness-raising" drugs have turned out to have distinct disadvantages such as residual effects and psychological and physical dependency as well as the required concentration of energy upon securing them. One example of youth seeking a natural high through religion is a return to evangelical faiths exemplified in the "Jesus movement".

However, some young people think they should always be in a euphoric state to maintain that high. Then, they pull back and seek other outlets.

In the *Electric Kool Aid Acid Test*, a book which was popular in the 1960s, Thomas Wolfe traces one far-out group's experimentation with drugs and sounds. The group members tried to attain an ultimate state of communion with each other. Then they moved beyond the use of drugs and tried to relate to each other without drugs. This communion was achieved; however, it made all those in the drug cult, who considered the leader to be their own personal guru, feel angry and cheated.

So, too, have many young adults sought to break the barrier that keeps them from spiritual growth. Some, unfortunately, have been lured into harmful religious groups, but others have sought and found a faith different from their parents, one which better answers the children's needs.

If your adult child has joined a detrimental religious cult, you should seek professional psychological and legal counseling as to how best to intervene.

Let's take a closer look at some of the influences on spiritual matters today in North America. Early reports on the use of psychedelic drugs seemed to affirm that people could expand their consciousness through artificial means. The reports were based upon claims of losing oneself in a greater span of consciousness. Later reports confirmed that the brain was affected detrimentally. Those seekers of an expanded consciousness then sought the sense of "being one with the universe," as offered by Eastern practitioners of meditation.

Yet this did not work for everyone and some people looked for other answers, greater, energized communion with others through intensive training and practice.

The promise of finding greater meaning in life rather than being "a ghost in a machine" as Arthur Koestler had defined modern man, is a meaningful goal which promises serenity and equanimity.

One form of higher spiritual experience has been called "peak experiences." Just as individuals experience intense inward forces, resulting in the blues, so, too, do people report peak experiences. These result from powerful outward or inward forces, and increase the possibility of extended psychological growth.

But an isolated peak experience may not have a permanent influence. Since its very nature is transitory, it's end result can be bewilderment; after *the* peaking, the person may feel let down and return to a lower level of psychological growth.

Young individuals may then search out circumstances which facilitate a repeat of the peak experience, or other techniques claiming to offer similar "highs." This may be drugs, meditation, or spiritual or religious organizations.

According to psychologist Abraham Maslow, the peak experience is one in which the person feels ecstasy. It has been described as a single most joyous, happiest, most blissful moment in one's life.

Through extensive interviewing, Maslow and his colleagues discovered that many people had experienced moments of ecstasy that could be classified as peak experiences but did not talk about them: they felt embarrassed or that the feelings were too private to be shared. The psychologists also discovered that the list of what triggers the moments is extensive. Two recurrent themes stuck out: music and sex. Experiences of true excellence, perfection, movement toward perfect justice or values—in many different areas—produced ecstatic experiences.

Natural childbirth can evoke a peak experience; some mothers describe it in mystical terms. Soon, perhaps, fathers who are present at birth can be encouraged to reveal their reactions in similar terms.

Music and art have evoked astounding metaphysical reactions, as have dance and rhythm.

The peak experiences, Maslow stated, have important consequences for our emotional system, although no one understands exactly why. At such times, people become more intensively aware of themselves, others, and their surroundings.

Not only personal and artistic moments, but other experiences, can be the basis for peaking. People can get turned on to mathematics and find a sudden joyousness in resolving an equation. Scientists looking through a microscope may suddenly see things in a different way, have a revelation, a moment of insight and ecstasy.

Getting people to describe their experiences in moments of particularly high emotion can provide clues to motivation, inner potential, and problem solving. Maslow questioned about *how* people felt differently, how the world looked differently, how people changed because of the experience, and what the impulses were.

When people feel expansion, they become more involved in the world and contribute more to it.

As an individual's psychological spiral expands, the possibility of his or her encountering a peak or transpersonal experience increases. The latter is defined as extending consciousness beyond the usual boundaries of ego, time, and space. The more receptive and trained a person is in allowing such experiences to happen, the greater the variation that is possible.

It has been said that everyone has the potential for achieving such higher states of consciousness built into the nervous system. However, the demands of everyday life may capture all of a person's attention so that the person's full creative potential is never reached.

Human beings have minds whose capability

far exceeds serving as switchboards for behavior; they have the capabilities of understanding and of intuitive interaction. To achieve the highest forms of interaction, humans have to be aware of and pay attention to their insights and experiences.

Through conscious effort, humans can develop formerly unknown capabilities. One means is joining and enhancing their human relations in groups. A second conscious effort is cultivating direction of personality energies through meditation.

A bridge is thus constructed between a person's superconscious and conscious selves. This type of mental functioning is different from abstract thinking and begins with intuition. Intuition is a link between the conscious and higher states. The energy of such a state has physical, emotional and mental components.

Belief in the spiritual side of human nature can be a source of strength. Many people seek a personally meaningful way of achieving some type of higher communion. The search has involved philosophers since earliest times; and there are no answers. Yet if parents want to help develop a spiritual dimension in their children they can:

1. *Help young adults articulate peak experiences.* Because young people find such experiences embarrassing to admit, and some emotions difficult to describe, they will let the daily chores of life capture their whole attention. Parents who wonder aloud about peak experiences with their young adults help focus attention beyond those barriers.

2. *Divulge their own struggles with transcending*

the mundane. When one person admits to some esoteric experience, sometimes others shyly reveal their own.

3. *Give positive, rather than negative, feedback about new techniques for communicating that religious sects develop that are relevant to the younger generations.* That is not to say that cults that exploit youth by hypnotic methods and complete obedience and strange practices are recommended, but that some changes in religious services can be productive. For instance, transcendental meditation can be a positive spiritual exercise. Or one can use it as a selfish excuse for abdicating responsibility.

Go with the young adult and seek to understand the religious or spiritual experience which is meaningful for him or her. What has meaning for a parent may not for the grown child; but mutual respect for the means of meeting spiritual needs can be achieved. Each person, in sum, has to look inward in order to look outward, to move from selfishness to selflessness. It can be an area of communion with self, others, and the world.

4. *Reflect what the young person is feeling and experiencing during the struggle to describe the event.* Sometimes the most help a parent can give is simply to respond in terms that reveal an attempt to understand the child—listening and joining as best as possible in comprehending the experience. Talking over dreams and contemplative moments might also be part of that shared experience. Grasping another per-

son's perception of a mystical experience is possible even without full approval. This reflective listening was described in depth in an earlier chapter.

The young person who has found a spiritual strength—or is still seeking one, perhaps by visiting with one group after another—is no different from people who for hundreds of generations have sought spiritual well-being. The freedom to choose one's faith is part of our heritage. To accord that right to our children may be difficult but, in the end, rewarding.

CHAPTER EIGHT

HOW TO DEAL WITH MATERIALISTIC GROWN CHILDREN

"Three times I thought my financial responsibility to my children had ended and they were finally going to be independent; when they got out of school, when they got jobs, and when they married and settled down. All three times I was wrong. They always ask me for a down payment or a loan—which is never repaid—or a co-signature for a loan," complained Mrs. Lefebre to her friend. "They cannot seem to become solvent. They say that the world is going to hell in a handbasket and they intend to enjoy life while they can."

A feeling of *anomie,* or listlessness and lack of control over events, deters psychological growth. Young people who take a hedonistic view of life— living for pleasures and immediate gratification—

have not had rewarding experiences with behaving otherwise.

The path to psychological well-being is not the same for any two people. Each person experiences unique forces acting with varying degrees of strength at different times.

Some individuals require more experiences to attain a degree of psychological growth similar to those of others. A frenetic involvement with instant gratification actually results in a slower pace of psychological growth (fewer coils). The person is dizzily covering ground, but is like a gyroscope spinning in place. A person can change and experience growth.

The closer the coils are to the central vertical axis, the more secure the person may feel because he or she needs to face fewer challenges and experiences. This is represented by less distance travelled along the spiral. This narrow distance is a reaction to the "pain" of growth, for it serves to obscure, ease, or delay the pain.

Seeking material possessions is another salve. With limited psychological growth, the person's needs are more infantile. He or she tries to find self-identity in possessions.

Young children's attachment to toys reflect this limited understanding. In adolescents and adults, clothes and automobiles may replace the toys. These precious possessions function as security blankets. If one looks at what was happening in the world when people now in their late teens, twenties, and thirties were born, diapered, shod, and sent off to kindergarten, their desire for warmth is understandable. First was the Cold War. Spies and war criminals stood trial and were executed. Vietnam claimed some

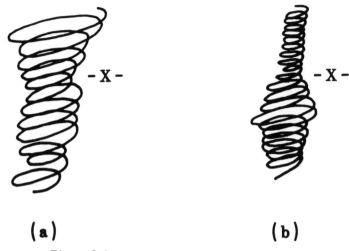

(a)   **(b)**

Figure 8-1
Two psychological spirals which were on similar paths of growth. (a) was able to assimilate into the growth pattern the occurrence at time "x". (b) experienced too much pain or shock at time "x" and regressed to the more secure but less psychologically healthy levels experienced earlier in life.

of our finest young people. Others marched and revolted. Witch hunts brewed suspicion. Floating anxiety and alienation clouded the air.

Also, many children grew up surrounded by and expecting luxuries. These represented significant achievements to the parents, but were taken as part of the environment by the youngsters.

This has resulted in modes of behavior widespread among today's young adults: avoidance and separateness.

Avoidance

Instant gratification of desires and pleasure-seeking existence served to keep young people so busy that they did not have to deal with more complex needs. Having desires met instantly was a luxury parents enjoyed providing to their young people. The "My-kid-is-never-going-to-have-to-do-without-the-things-I-did" syndrome escalated.

Teaching children to delay gratification in order to attain a larger, long-range, or aspired-for goal is difficult. Moreover, while aspiration defined in terms of objects is clear, aspiration defined as spiritual, mental, and physical growth is harder to pin down, takes longer to wrestle with, and demands placing one's energies into getting the shoulder to the wheel in order to achieve what the neighbors cannot see.

Many of the fast food generation avoid dealing with the challenges involved in attaining psychological growth. However, the price is often disquietude and emptiness.

Separateness.

People who do not give up childish things and ways of thinking become grown, but not grown-up. They continue to have the irrational beliefs and thoughts of childhood.

Some people are so enmeshed in getting the luxuries offered in their environment that their view of self is physically and emotionally linked to the environment; their psychological spiral is very narrow. They see material possessions as representing self or they must constantly receive support and affection from others in a one-way, infantile relationship.

To move toward growth, the self has to be viewed as separate but interacting with the environment. The self has to be distinguished from things and other people. Psychologically mature adults find comfort in solitariness and are not lonely and uneasy when alone. Avoiding the pain of growth can account for personality fixation at a childish level. Certain young adults, when their basic needs such as food and shelter are met, are unwilling or too frustrated to venture outward. To meet higher-level needs, one must continually extend consciousness. Then, as one grows psychologically, one is prepared to meet and welcome greater spiritual growth. Without some psychological growth, it is not possible to move beyond gratifying the more basic needs. Such unrealized persons remain immersed in gratifying childlike needs. The maturing person is always in the process of becoming, of growing.

If an individual is easily frustrated by attempts to move outward, he or she might retreat, as shown in Figure 8-2. If an individual places more emphasis upon greater growth, he or she can sometimes move on rapidly, as shown in (b), or might have to go more slowly (c).

Mrs. Lefebre's (the woman spoken of at the beginning of this chapter) children may be frantically trying to stave off their feelings of lack of control over outside forces. Admittedly, there are occasions when a person is at the mercy of day-to-day survival; at the mercy of some greater authority figure, such as a tyrannical teacher or dictatorial boss, too many appointments, too many family demands for money, the newsworthy shenanigans of a relative, a nationwide recession, a world gone nuclear war-crazy. And under

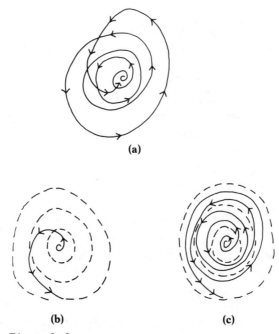

(a)

(b)   (c)

Figure 8–2
Three spirals illustrate attempts to grow beyond environment.
(a) Attempting to move outward, frustration causes retreat
and return to previous levels. (b) Needs met by the environment, individual easily moves outward. (c) Moving outward
is difficult, but the individual persists.

such circumstances, people are deeply upset and react almost automatically, and have little time to
weigh their opinions about their other choices.

Not all things and events can be controlled by
individuals. The cue is the word "time": people can
propitiously guard time to consider their options.

A person can control a helpless attitude. Our
attitudes are under our control. For example, the way

a young person considers a problem can be discussed and explored. Perhaps the person is taking things too personally, allowing threat to stunt the growth potential of an experience.

When your young adult feels pressured by time constraints and too many duties, teach him or her to set watches ahead ten minutes. Setting the clock ahead also gives breathing room to reduce feelings of being on a treadmill.

Show your young adult how to take "a time out" break of short duration during which to exercise, take a walk, or meditate.

In addition, suggest that *the person can change part of the environment.* Switching schools or jobs, moving to another locale, paying into a savings account as though it were a monthly statement, doing tasks for the community, writing letters of support and protest, and joining action groups are ways to effect change in one's life. Show the young adult how . Remember, plans for change take a commitment of time.

Also, steps to commit time, change one's own attitudes, and change the environment have to be accompanied by positive feedback from significant others. Perhaps Mrs. Lefebre actually enjoys—and therefore reinforces—the grown children's claims on her finances. She *could* say "no."

When you have given your child positive feedback it is time to *examine goals* with him or her. Chapter Four suggests several ways of encouraging a healthy look at where young adults are going and how they are going to get there. Because the need for reflective periods in the early stages of life are often not part of the young person's decision-making process, such periods must be planned for and considered. Often a parent can get the maturing adult away from his or her environment for an afternoon or evening to review the person's ideas and thoughts about life, particularly its meaning and purpose.

CHAPTER NINE

CONFLICT OVER MONEY

"Our teenaged boys spend most of their free time at the nearby shopping mall. Although they both have weekend jobs, they don't help out at home, nor do they save a cent. Everything they make goes for stereo tapes, Don Johnson lookalike clothes and their car. Meanwhile, my husband and I skrimp to put aside money for their future educations," complained Joan Walters.

"My husband and I are struggling with our twenty-year-old right now," added Vera Schmidt. "Last year he quit the university and decided that he'd go to California for a few weeks' vacation. We thought that would allow him some time to straighten his life out. He came home broke and hasn't been able to find any kind of work which he finds acceptable. We've threatened to move him out, but we're concerned that he'd go right down the drain, maybe into a life of drugs or something."

"I have a similar concern with our daughter. She's unhappy in her marriage and has talked to us about leaving her husband. Since she doesn't have a full-time job, she asked us if she and her five-month-old could move in with us. Our concern is that once she moves in we would be supporting them both and providing free babysitting. What do you think we should do?" asked Betty Mills.

An old maxim was:

Use it up
Wear it out
Fix it up or
Do without.

This is still a wise philosophy. Without such an outlook, our children will never find out how *unlimited* is their potential for managing life without outside financial help.

A primary goal of parenting is to raise children who can become financially independent and live responsible lives. Adult children who have remained dependent on the family may drain it both emotionally and financially. In previous generations the process of launching children was generally more clear cut and less stressful. Career options provided alternative choices and flexibility which are often not available for today's young adults. Completion of high school or university no longer has the job guarantees of the past. Difficulty in knowing what career to pursue has left many young people confused, frustrated, and disillusioned. Individuals who have pursued careers have found it difficult to attain financial independence through suitable employment, even after completing appropriate training.

Some parents have felt that their children were launched and finding their way in the world only to be confronted with grown children on their doorstep. Caught by economic fluctuations, many have experienced layoffs and loss of income. Some return home following a marriage breakdown, seeking emotional and financial support which had been provided during earlier years. Others use home as a respite during periods of transition from one life style to another, such as the military to civilian. During these times parents may watch helplessly, wondering where to turn and what to do. Very few parents have the unlimited financial resources or housing space. Many have worked hard looking forward to child-free days. During this phase they believe they will be able to concern themselves primarily with their own needs and wants, focusing on husband-wife relationships, career aspirations, and leisure activities. Parents may experience feelings of ambivalence and frustration as they attempt to successfully launch their young adults and find that these children try to return to dependent children roles.

The issue of financial independence and responsibility can become a major source of concern and conflict between parents and their maturing children.

In a society which has become increasingly materialistic, it is not surprising that money and its value have become major sources of conflict.

Ideally, parents are able to teach their children how to adjust to frustration by tolerance throughout the child's early life. The knick-knacks on the shelf weren't available to the infant for touching or playing. The latest toy seen on the Saturday morning cartoon shows by the eight-year-old wasn't always purchased. For a sixteen-year-old the family auto has to prove sufficient, rather than having his or her own car. Through such incremental doses of frustration, particularly on monetary issues, the child's tolerance to the realities of life may be learned.

A positive attitude toward delayed gratification is developed through years of parental effort. When maturing children are teenagers in high school the pros and cons of post-secondary education should be weighed, family finances discussed in terms of balancing the impulse for new cars, expensive clothes, and extra money with the benefits of saving. Teenagers are, in reality, individuals in transition. Some children are, at this stage, more capable of making financial decisions than others.

SPENDING MONEY

All children benefit from the experience of handling money for themselves. Using money is the only way to learn the financial facts of life.

Regular spending money is a preferable way to meet the child's needs—both his practical need for money and the emotional need for independence. The amount of allowance should be realistically related to the child's needs. By the time youngsters are in high school they should be ready to budget on a monthly basis. What is important is consistency. Since the child has a big stake in the decision as to how much, he is more likely to be satisfied if he had a voice in the decision making. The ground rules should be laid and the expectations of both parents and child gotten out into the open. Review the decision regularly, at least every few months, and certainly annually. Allowances are learning tools to manage money. Tying money to behavior conveys the impression that approval can be bought. This is not a good idea. Set reasonable limits based on your family's values and allow children to develop their independence gradually as they mature.

Often children within the same household do not share similar views of material needs. Sometimes parent-child conflicts are enflamed by vastly differing views of the worth of a dollar, not only between generations but between siblings. What worked well for one child may not have the same results with another child. Many parents have expressed the concern that the youngest child is considerably more difficult to reason with and raise. For others it has been the oldest or the middle. The point is that sometimes parenting techniques do yield vastly differing results. This has baffled more than one set of parents.

Adult children who have experienced sufficient psychological growth can be expected to assume financial responsibilities and independence comparatively easier than less stable siblings. To expect even grown children to assume control over age-appropriate tasks when they have not demonstrated such maturity is possibly asking the impossible. It further risks another negative experience being added to the list of events composing the person's self-image. For example, it may be unwise to provide such costly items as an automobile of their own to children who have not consistently demonstrated responsible behavior. Aside from the constraints of the law, such items require that the individual monitor water in the summer and antifreeze in the winter, and oil level throughout the year.

Initially, a grown child may best demonstrate his or her maturity on smaller tasks and less costly items which don't require as much family investment. For children who have demonstrated emotional maturity, pressure to assume monetary independence can be an outward force resulting in greater psychological growth. But, attempts at forcing independence financially or psychologically may prove very dangerous when dealing with less psychologically stable individuals. For those individuals whose psychological development has not expanded to the same extent, even less pressure may prove very threatening, interpreted as an inward pull. The result is that the grown child may regress inward to such an extent that emotional health and stability, as well as financial independence, are in jeopardy. Reasonably stable and well balanced parents, who have been quite successful coping with life, may fail to understand and appreciate the difficulty that some grown children have in handling what may seem routine tasks. When attempting to shift financial responsibility to less stable children, having them accept small responsibilities may be advisable, particularly in the early phases. Incremental increases in expectations should then be monitored. When working with highly irresponsible or depressed grown children, consultation with appropriate professionals is advisable.

EMPLOYMENT

The groundwork for parent-child relationships involving monetary responsibility is often laid early. The first work most kids do consists of household chores. They take the garbage out, set and clear the

table, do the dishes, are more or less responsible for keeping their rooms neat. These jobs need doing and children are part of the family. It is important to give children some interesting tasks instead of the annoying ones that parents don't want to do. Children like variety as much as adults do. Often doing tasks for a neighbor rather than for family gives maturing children a feel of real responsibility and develops the sense of accountability. The surest road to independence is a clear understanding of real work and real earnings. Sometimes such jobs have negative instead of positive effects. Despite the fact that it is difficult to be highly successful on several fronts, many teenagers still attempt more than they can handle. It takes an exceptional teenager to succeed at work, school, sports, and dating. The stress involved may not be growth producing. School is still the child's most important responsibility, but schoolwork often suffers, jeopardizing future options. However, if a child is doing well at school, has ample time for recreation, can fit in his household chores, and is eager to work, work can offer opportunities for early lessons in independence.

Indeed, volunteer jobs offer some of the same benefits and are often easier to secure, especially for younger teens. The important thing is that maturing children learn to fulfill their commitments. Accountability is inherent in the assignments, and parents must allow children to take responsibility themselves. Overprotection is maturity's worst enemy.

Parents should try, as children mature, to discuss children's earnings and expenditures and to supervise children's activities whether or not they earn money.

If parents act as independent financial advisors, allowing their children more and more responsibility to develop their value systems, the groundwork for complete independence is laid. Nevertheless, the extra cash teenagers earn sometimes encourages teenagers to be more consumer oriented, spending their earnings on clothing, autos, records, and other luxuries which their peers view as valuable. Advertisers are well aware of this disposable income and attempt to provide goods and services appealing to youth. The result is often that teens save little. Valuable lessons regarding budgeting and saving for university or future security are often missed.

A dialogue between a high school teacher and student provides some insight as to where the money from part-time employment may go:

> *Teacher:* "Bill, I've noticed that your grades seem to be slipping."
>
> *Student:* "Yes, I've been working more lately."
>
> *Teacher:* "Oh, is there any special reason why you've been working more?"
>
> *Student:* "Yes, I need to pay the car insurance for my car."
>
> *Teacher:* "Well, why do you need a car?"
>
> *Student:* "So I can get back and forth to work."

Moreover, in many cases the financial independence provided by part-time work has not been accompanied by an understanding or appreciation of saving. On the other hand, those children who are supported by their parents until the end of high school may also fail to develop an appreciation for the work behind the money flowing into the family. Family budgets, like sex, are often not openly discussed with maturing children. Even when they are, children often do not appreciate parents' desire to save for the future. Instead children may see the cash flow into their homes as part of their disposable income, in much the same way they see the money from their part-time work. Herein lies a major source of conflict in the parent-child relationship.

In an effort to provide greater understanding of the costs of maintaining a family, even young children should be brought into discussions of family finances. The goal is to develop an appreciation for daily costs experienced by a family. Long-term expenditures, such as the home and auto purchases, should be included. The need to save for short-term expenses, such as auto insurance and new clothing, should be discussed with the children, ideally from an early age. The wisdom of long-term investments may not be fully appreciated even by grown children, but the seed for thought should be planted early.

As part of the discussion of family finances the budgeting of part-time earnings should be considered. Grown children should realize that there will be a variety of expenditures to take into account. In particular, saving for post-secondary expenses (tuition, room and board, books, etc.) may be included in a budget.

In the process of working the student may have access to a car, not only for work but for socializing. However, by the time insurance, gas, and maintenance have been paid very little may have been saved from the earnings. For many youths parental encouragement to secure part-time employment has produced little more than good times for the present. Without saving for the future or contributing to the family, many teenagers may become more now-oriented and self-centered, expecting a continuous cash flow with little responsibilities. An opportunity to develop a sense of delayed gratification has been lost.

Further, in pursuit of part-time employment involvement in sports and other wholesome extracurricular activities, such as debate, community projects, and drama, are limited. Such involvement usually develops self-discipline and a sense of commitment to activities with non-monetary rewards, and they have traditionally provided opportunities for teenagers to grow socially and psychologically.

The disposable income of grown children who choose to work but live at home sometimes exceeds that of their parents. It is not uncommon for these young adults to be driving their own new cars, wearing expensive clothing, and traveling to places their parents have yet to consider. For these grown children the discussion of the family budget could include small amounts being paid toward expenses incurred in maintaining the grown child such as room and board, transportation, education. Some parents clearly establish expectations for room and board. For example, when the grown child is no longer in school as a full-time student or achieving at a satisfactory level, then the charges may begin to accumulate. Even though employment hasn't been secured, payments are still not forgiven.

Summer breaks may be an exception, provided adequate savings are budgeted for a return to school in the fall. The purpose of these guidelines is to help develop a realization that all income is not disposable and with age comes added responsibilities. After all it would seem ironic for the grown children to be living the "good life" while their parents struggled to maintain them.

LOANS AND GIFTS TO GROWN CHILDREN

Opening a bank account serves as an introduction to money lending institutions. One advantage of encouraging children as they enter adolescence and beyond to maintain a personal bank account is that overdrafts are a matter between the bank and the account holder. This avoids a potential conflict over parent-child loans which can develop into a prolonged source of aggravation. Despite the fact that a child may have demonstrated social responsibility, many parents make the mistake of lending money in large amounts to their children. Some large debts accumulate as a series of small debts over a period of time. In other cases the parents lend large amounts for major purchases such as a stereo system, car, or mortgages toward the purchase of a home. Parents may well consider encouraging their grown children to arrange loans from lending institutions. In such cases any problems involving repayment are a matter out of the hands of the parents. An obvious exception is for parents who are financially able to absorb any failure to repay.

Parents who are unable to resist assisting their

grown children or who decide to provide financial assistance should consider formalizing such loans. Just as lending institutions require a credit rating, parents who feel financially comfortable enough to lend money to their children may wish to begin with small loans of ten to fifty dollars. If the grown child is unable to repay such small loans under agreed-upon conditions and on a schedule, then a clear message is being sent to the parents. For children without a proven financial track record, larger loans such as $8,000 for a car or $100,000 for a home may well be interpreted as a gift, as repayment may be an unrealistic expectation. In an effort to avoid possible misunderstandings, parents may consider formalizing loans in writing with possible consultation with a lawyer. Interest rates could be set below those charged at banks. Any grown child who objects to such procedures should be encouraged to explore the conditions offered by the formal lending institutions. A visit to a local bank may prove valuable and develop an appreciation for any parental considerations.

Parents should handle monetary issues within their financial capabilities and within a level of commitment that they feel comfortable both financially and emotionally. Children of all ages are capable of manipulating their parents on a wide variety of issues, not just monetary. A typical technique involves the sentences beginning "Well, everybody's doing, going, or getting something paid for by their parents." Children may not like to hear that different parents respond differently, but this is in fact a reality of life. Explanations of parental views and stands need not be lengthy. Rational and logical arguments often fail to achieve their purpose of convincing grown children, and for every logical reason or example the parents give the child may be able to quickly counter. State your position firmly and succinctly. Another reason for formalizing the conditions of loans or gifts is that any ambiguity is hopefully minimized. Parents are again cautioned to give and provide within their means. Any conditions that parents wish to place on loans and gifts should be very clear. For example, if a parent gives a high school graduate an automobile for graduation without any conditions then the grown child is free to do with the car as he or she wishes. If finances become tight during the first year of college or a trip to Europe needs to be financed, then the sale of an $8,000 car for $4,000 by the young adult may leave the parents with little recourse unless they had spelled out clearly what could be done with the car. Similarly, parents who provide a piano for their child to play and practice on need to clarify whether or not the piano is the property of the child or whether upon termination of playing the piano reverts back to the parents for their disposal. Formalizing such loans and gifts may seem too business-like for most parents and lacking in family trust. However, more than one parent has felt crushed and betrayed for years at what seemed to be inconsiderate behavior on the part of a grown child. Open, honest communication, although awkard during the early stages, may do much to promote a strong, long-lasting relationship based on clear understanding. Although weaning a grown child from financial dependence can prove trying, parents are encouraged to make their decisions free of guilt, realizing that grown children must learn to be independent if they are to become self-actualized, productive adults.

CHAPTER TEN

MORAL STANDARDS AND THE ADULT CHILD

"My big problem is that my thirty-one-year-old daughter is living with a fellow and wants to bring him home for Thanksgiving, and my other daughter's daughter, who is sixteen—my granddaughter—wants me to go with her to get birth control pills, since she doesn't have an allowance and is afraid to ask her mother for them. My two daughters snub each other. What a mess this holiday is going to be," said Mrs. Feldshuh wearily.

"That's minor. My son will end up hitting his wife, his kids and ME before it's all over," moaned Mrs. Smythe.

Standards of morality have changed in the past twenty-five years. This change is partially a reaction against the traditional double standard, where it was all right for men to have sexual intercourse, but not women. Another change has been brought about by the birth control pill, and still another by the increase in the number of self-supporting men and women.

Adolescents are reaching puberty at younger and younger ages; this is the result of better diet and temperature controls in our living spaces. At the same time, adolescents are called upon less and less to contribute to the family's survival and well-being. They are kept in adolescent limbo until the age of majority (eighteen to twenty-one). They have money, cars, and distorted media expressions of what is masculine and feminine. Parents are cautioned by experts not to inhibit sexual development, but urged to guide the morality of the young. However, responsibility is still a key issue in regard to morality.

Morality is now in the hands of the local community, and different areas of the continent define proper behavior in different ways. Moreover, there are individual matters of conscience. Moral development is far broader than the issues of sexuality. There are ethical approaches to the questions about moral development, there are dictates of right and wrong from self-declared authorities, and there are developmental approaches.

Whatever approach a community uses, the predominant values of the society in a given locale will influence the young adult's attitude regarding what is illegal and immoral. The attitudes will also be influenced by songs and video cassettes, movies, television, books, and magazines aimed at the particular age group.

Although specific sexual patterns have differed across the centuries, two universal imperatives, as proposed by philosopher Immanuel Kant, are still valid:

Treat other people as an ends, not as means.
Behave as you would have everyone behave in a similar circumstance.

Reports indicate that the sexual revolution is over, people have found one-night stands less satisfying than establishing long-term, intimate relationships and have become aware of the physiological diseases which are sometimes the product of such liaisons. Moreover, people have discovered that treating other people as a "means" and acting upon one's own immediate desires, regardless of the outcome, have not proven meaningful. Respecting other people and building a relationship or family life for one's own and society's benefit are more worthwhile. Both women and men are tired of being exploited.

Similar to the developmental stages of childhood through to adulthood, stages of moral development also grow outward. Figure 10–1 shows the developmental, and somewhat age-related developmental stages, for males and females (from Kohlberg and Gilligan).

Female Moral Development. Because of the importance to women of relationships with other people, females tend to interpret moral dilemmas in terms of how a situation affects the people involved. "Right" and "wrong" are attenuated by what would happen to an important relationship, such as one between husband and wife.

For example, Carole Gilligan pointed out in *In A Different Voice* that women describe their moral development in concepts of fairness and equity. Becoming more mature in judgment begins with a concern for individual survival, which is a kind of selfish-

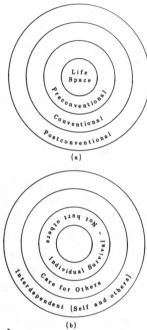

(a)

(b)

Figure 10–1
Stages of moral development differ for (a) men and (b) women.

ness, and proceeds through taking responsibility for others to a balance between responsibility to self as well as others. For most women care and responsibility in relationships are of paramount importance.

Typically, women move from principle not to hurt others to recognition that sustaining relationships requires acting responsively to self and others.

Male Moral Development. For males, the *preconventional* level is usually found in youngsters up to age twelve. Typically, male children have a punishment-and-obedience orientation and then a "what's-in-it-for-me" attitude.

The second level, *conventional*, is first characterized by a good-boy-nice-girl orientation. This is an attitude usually found in teens. The next stage at this level has a law-and-order orientation; "It's against the law, that's why you mustn't." The third level is the *post-conventional*, found in some adult men. Here a socially contractual, legalistic orientation is found, as well as a grander, universal, ethical principle orientation. The latter reveals concern for humanity above concern for one's self.

The latter three stages (last half of level two and all of level three) may be interchangeable, depending upon the situation. As a person develops morally, the latter stages include experience with the lower stages. The lower stages may, therefore, be invoked in particular situations.

Exposure to people at a higher stage seems to provide a model that enables those stranded in a lower level to move upward. Lawrence Kohlberg, who developed and studied this paradigm, placed people who resolved dilemmas in terms of the *intent* of the person committing a certain act higher on the scale than he did those who replied in terms of the enormity of a situation—such as a large vase broken accidentally versus a small vase broken on purpose.

When family members, peers, and the community and media try to examine the intent and judge the aptness of behavior upon intent, then higher levels are modelled. If punishment swiftly follows an act or bribery used for "good" behavior, then lower levels of action persist.

Inconsistencies abound. An argument has raged for many years through the United States over whether the death penalty is a deterrent to crimes such as murder. It is said that people on death row represent an uneven administration of "justice"; their sentences were based more upon racial factors and low socioeconomic status than upon the severity of their crimes. Similarly, the death penalty for rape was hard for juries to administer in a society that used such colloquialisms as "nice girls don't get raped" and "women will lie." Today, new graduated laws which take into consideration degrees of assault have been passed. Sentences are slowly being revised to more adequately serve a deterrent purpose and the protection of society.

Concern for victims is on the upswing. Support groups, crisis centers, special training of legal, medical, and police professionals are attempting to protect the rights of victims and their families as well as the accused.

Society is responding to needs, but basic questions remain. How does conscience develop? How can healthy development be furthered? What does a parent do with a grown child who seems stuck in a childish stage of moral and ethical behavior?

As shown in Figure 10–2, some people move unerringly into upper stages; others have more difficulty.

A conscience develops through a realization that one's actions affect others. When parents discuss with their children how behavior affects others, and help them observe people who act in a concerned manner toward other human beings, young people grow morally. Two key attitudes that parents should encourage in their children are empathy and the idea that thinking can change.

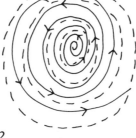

Figure 10–2
Two psychological spirals demonstrating differing experiences and patterns through which people move while progressing from one level of moral development to another. The spiral may have been influenced by such factors as life experiences, society, and home environment—including the parents' level of moral development.

EMPATHY

At very young ages, some children show empathy—the human ability to realize another person is in distress. While this capacity may later become hidden under selfish and frustrating conditions, it still exists.

Empathy can be modelled by concerned parents. Their actions and descriptions of their actions toward others should be overt. The model of helping and protecting other people is important.

Young persons should be able to recognize how their actions affect others.

Parents may have to use powerful, assertive approaches that combine affection with the threat of withdrawing love to get through to someone who has exhibited behavior that threatens to exploit other people. Arousing some anxiety may enable the young adult to reconsider and change such behavior. In addition, if the young adult is taught to act as though an authority is present at times of choice between behaviors, faulty behavior patterns can be changed. However, techniques that foster the development of self discipline need to be instituted as soon as possible.

THINKING CAN CHANGE

New ideas and issues concerning other people's rights and morality problems are common at the adolescent stage. New information and taking another person's perspective can effect a movement upward on the moral development scale. And these higher levels involve change in reasoning and action when confronted with moral dilemmas.

To help young adults improve their moral behavior and better understand their moral responsibility, information has to be disclosed, explained, and repeated. It can be divulged through reading, discussion of events, or speculations. When a young adult is confronted with a personal dilemma, that threat and all its possible solutions offer parents an opportunity to effect a change of thinking to a more compassionate level. Psychological growth includes moral development. Parents can help young adults observe how their behavior affects others and how their attitudes can change through several means. While using parental affection and the threat of withdrawing it can force the young adult to confront problems, modelling a pro-social concern for others proclaims the correct approach. Encouraging the grown child to consider how behavior affects others permits correction in his or her internal directives for behavior. Personal dilemmas and sought information pose teachable moments when parents can effectively intervene.

But, new behaviors are not likely to become learned behavior unless the young adult can effectively engage in changing past habits. Some approaches to this are:

Rehearsal. People who have learned a certain way for a long time do so automatically. If a new way of behaving is to seem feasible, the young adult has to practice it. Rehearsal of recurring interaction with other people and using new ways of handling that interaction are necessary. Parents can role-play better choices in the grown child's life-script by taking the part of the second person.

Several options should be tried. Next, the young adult can try out the new approaches. If something does not work, another option should be tried. In a given situation an individual has any number of responses possible and has to isolate those that work. Feedback from parents affirms positive change.

Relieving Frustration. If the volatile young adult is taking frustration out on other people, then other tactics for channeling the frustration must be found. Some people find a release in the use of words (better than administering beatings). Others need a physical release—some type of activity such as sports, hard labor, or punching a bag.

Reciprocal Role-Taking. Perhaps the young adult simply is ignorant of the effects of his or her behavior upon other people. In this case, the parent can take the grown child's role and have the young adult rehearse the responses, feelings, and reactions of the second parties. After a scene has been replayed, the discussion should not end with the young adult being permitted to express selfish perceptions of the second party, although this reporting is the first and natural thing to do: the discussion should continue until the young adult actually perceives how other people feel.

Non-Deludedness. All of these ideas are means of enhancing the grown child's moral comprehension. Practical knowledge comes from maturation, instructions, thinking, and understanding how behavior affects other people. Young adults can discipline themselves by thinking about their behavior and by using new options until they become automatic. They can learn to discriminate between proper and improper behavior toward others. Do not be part of a self-centered youg adults' desire to delude himself or herself into thinking that his or her needs and problems take precedence over what happens to others. "No man in an island."

CHAPTER ELEVEN

TEACHING THE GROWN CHILD TO DEAL WITH DEATH

"I cannot stop grieving over the death of my granddaughter. She was so young. She had so much going for her. I am just no help at all to my son and his family," said Mrs. Bass.

"I feel the loss of my girlfriend as keenly as her parents do," wept Bob Piccolo. "I've read the Bible, but I can't relate it to her being gone."

"Our son just died. His brother seems to blame himself and us," said Mr. Horowitz.

Accepting the concept of death can be considered the final phase in psychological growth. Some religions emphasize attainment of a paradisical afterlife as the sole reason for living a good life on earth. Others emphasize that living a good life is the main purpose of being on earth.

Yet, not all people young or old believe in immortality or can take comfort in the beliefs of religion.

The main thing is that death is a part of life. As we live longer and the ritualistic behaviors surrounding death have removed care of the dying from our homes, children and adults seldom know how to deal with death. Young adults, who lose a sibling, child, or parent have seldom observed the processes of grief, nor do they accept the platitude that death is a part of life. Fears of death can also stalk the young threatened by crazed killers, as when the school children in Atlanta knew an unknown assailant was lurking somewhere in the neighborhood.

Conversely, so much violent death is being viewed on television that for some young adults death may be experienced as unreal and seen as distant, impersonal, and removed from one's own concerns.

Fears and procedures surrounding death should be aired and discussed with your children. The soft breath of reason can overcome fears or impersonal views of death. When death comes to an older person, our attitudes to it are bound up with society's views of older persons: they may be left to die alone, with technical help provided, but without personal, emotional, or spiritual support. When death comes to a young person, attitudes are then intertwined with the worship of youth. The young person's potential, the sense of unfairness at a life ended that was scarcely begun, the intimate involvement of the family in raising the youth contribute to a sense of outrage at a young person taken in death by illness or accident.

In airing thoughts about death with their parents, young adults can learn to react with sorrow but reason to death. They can anticipate that those who have died will be commemorated and will be remembered with love and pleasant memories.

DEATH AND THE YOUNG ADULT

If the young adult is himself or herself gravely ill, sometimes the best approach is to listen to the concerns, to answer requests for information for existential or insoluble matters. Dying persons want information just as much as other family members do. When and how to deal with fears requires the ability to go beyond one's own needs and emotions to respond to the needs of others.

Of course, if the parent is too caught up in emotional reaction to his or her child's imminent death or to the philosophical questions involved, it is better to let someone else in the support network serve as a resource.

Kubler-Ross and others have furnished many commentaries on the stages that dying people may go through.

The first stage is *denial*, or, "This is not happening." Persons in this stage may act stoic and seek acknowledgment from others that this is not happening. They can discover their own strengths, share ideas, rearrange priorities, find new goals, or try to ignore the implications. It may be a long, waxing/waning experience, or a short one.

The second stage is *anger.* Critical comments

are levied at everyone and everything. Outrage may be followed by bitterness. The person looks for some reason for the "punishment" and finds it unfair. Blame, resentment, and guilt toward self or others are typical components. Parents can help to direct energy toward bettering conditions or working to help others.

The *bargaining* third stage is characterized by attempting some type of agreement. This may consist of prolonging acceptance of the loss until something (for example, a wedding, a graduation) occurs. The person also may rationalize that other people are in worse shape or that things could be personally worse.

The fourth stage, *depression*, sets in with a great sense of loss. The person is preoccupied with self. Withdrawing into self follows the admission that "Yes, it *is* I."

The fifth stage, *acceptance*, follows the emotional work that has gone before. It is a quiet resolution, almost devoid of labile feelings. The expectations are admitted and quietly faced.

Not all of these stages may be observed nor will they always occur in this order. We've described them here so that parents can try to recognize the particular stage the adult child is experiencing.

THE DEATH OF SOMEONE CLOSE

Grief over the death of someone close is expected, although our society does not furnish enough time for mourning. When a family member is terminally ill, the family members may anticipate grief and may have already dealt with some of the spiritual and frightening aspects ahead of time. In that case, the period of mourning may be less. The state of mourning usually lasts, however, for about a year. Rushing it by, insisting people get back into the normal routine without time for contemplation, is detrimental. It may prolong the process or add an unnecessary load on the person. The Irish wake and the Jewish *shiva* are excellent examples of approaches that enhance mental health. Such ritualistic celebrations are not self-indulgent, weak, nor disrespectful: they are agents of adjustment.

Most people's first reaction to the death of someone close is *shock*, with a numb feeling that may last from a little while to several weeks. During this stage, the supportive network has to handle details of burial, inheritance, belongings, bills, and visitors. Taking care of these details may be a useful demand on the attention of those most directly involved or may better be handled by others in the support network. Many ethnic groups have excellent support networks that automatically swing into action.

The second stage after "death of a significant other" is marked by *mental anguish, reliving scenes, depression,* and *aimlessness.* It often lasts up to ten weeks. There is a strong need of the most affected persons to have empathy and support to return to normal everyday life. Where families are scattered, this period may be experienced all alone, if the bereaved person does not seek solace or have a strong social network. Attempts should be made to fill the void in social support.

The last stage is one of *developing awareness.* New patterns of living are assimilated as recovery proceeds. The person needs social contacts in this period. A strong spiritual belief is a source of strength. The survivor often wishes to discuss views of life and death, or previous experiences with the person who died, and observe conclusions that have been drawn. This is a good time for parents and children to share their feelings about the meaning of life and death. This will be helpful to the adult child in later adjustment to other deaths, in many cases, the parents. The period of mourning, whether in anticipation of one's own or another's death or in dealing with another's death afterwards, lends itself to examination.

Before death, terminally ill patients often wish to review their lives. An empathetic listener can be a great support. Many young adults engage in much self examination during the stages following the death of a significant other. All members of a family can join in looking at what life means, how it should be lived, what is important. Learning how to share sorrow as well as joy helps young people gain new perspectives on the meanings of life.

Discuss with your child how psychological growth can emanate from new examination of one's own life after a loved one has died.

CHAPTER TWELVE

SEXUALITY AND LIFESTYLE CHOICES

"My granddaughter wants to go on the pill; that means she is promiscuous," moaned plain-featured Mrs. Feldshuh.

"Well, there can be worse things. My brother has just moved in with a guy and announced that they are both gay," said Joel Harris.

"One of my friends decided to have a baby and she is not married," petite and brown-haired Ms. Long confided.

The Census in 1980 showed a decline in the proportion of households that are family households. Among other changes, the number of unmarried couples living together constituted 3.5 percent of all couple households. This percentage was triple that found in the 1970 Census.

Our family system today is struggling with the

morality of sexuality. The younger generation is making choices that in previous decades were deemed disgraceful, and which today's parents, when younger adults, would never have even considered. Yet, the choices seem perfectly acceptable to their peers. Although young adults today have more options and the freedom to experiment with different types of relationships and lifestyles, many families have to struggle with shock at unexpected elements being introduced into their lives. Whatever the sexuality issue is, it affects the personal feelings of each family member in many new and different ways.

FAMILY AS RESOURCE

Any event that creates stress on a family is a crisis. The crisis is usually an event that the family has not handled before. It is a disruptive change that does not appear to be amenable to previous methods of resolution. No model exists for dealing with the stressful event.

The degree of intensity of a crisis depends upon both how the family construes the event and upon the strength of the family bonds. For example, if a family construes the stressor as one that was anticipated, the disruption will be less, and the intensity of the crisis less than for families to whom the disruption is abrupt. Moreover, when common interests, affection, strong kinship feelings from an extended network, and economic interdependence characterize the bonds between family members, then the family resources are greater and better able to withstand trauma.

Stronger family units will experience less stress, but some stress will still be present, because the members are powerless to prevent certain crises from happening. This is especially true when one family member decides upon a sexual lifestyle or choice which departs from family or societal norms. The terms commonly used by older adults to describe present-day choices reveal the pejorative nature of the sanctions: *premarital, shacking-up, acting-out* sexually, *queer,* and *unwed* mother/*unwed* father. Young adults, in contrast, look upon their choices as soaring acceptance of a joyful part of life. They see themselves as loving and human, not acting-out; as gay and willing to be so identified, not queer; and as caring parents, not unwed tramps.

Although parents may not approve of their adult children's sexual styles, they still have to come to terms with their disillusionment and with their children's freedom of choice—or prepare to lose their child. Parental expectations that a certain order exists are based upon their own acceptance of society's demands.

REACTIONS OF FAMILY MEMBERS

Any type of crisis or trauma can evoke emotional reactions. Losing a job, the break-up of a marriage, a family member marrying outside the ethnic group elicit crisis reactions. Intensified reactions can be anticipated when family members hear of a choice about sexuality that disrupts old traditions, and these parallel almost exactly the emotional stages of people faced with their own deaths.

One reaction is *denial,* or "This is not happening." The shock may be characterized by a numb feeling. Some parents or relatives may act stoic and hopeful and seek acknowledgement from others that this is not happening. On the positive side, people can discover their own strengths, share ideas, rearrange priorities, find new goals, or try to ignore the implications. It may be a long, waxing/waning experience, or a brief reaction.

Another reaction is *anger*. Mental anguish is turned outward. Parents direct critical, often hurtful, comments at everyone and everything. This may be followed by bitterness. Parents look for some reason why they're being "punished" and find it all unfair. Blame, resentment, and guilt regarding self or others are typical components.

The *bargaining* reaction is characterized by attempting some type of agreement. The bargain may be hidden and unspoken. Acceptance of the child's actions may be prolonged until something occurs (e.g., a wedding, a graduation). There may also be rationalization that other people are in worse shape, or that things could be worse.

A fourth reaction, *depression,* sets in when the parent feels a great sense of loss. The person becomes preoccupied with him- or herself. This usually follows the admission that, "Yes, it is I who has a child who has made that choice."

Finally, *acceptance* may and should occur after people have worked through their perceptions of the crisis. It is a quiet resolution, almost devoid of volatile feelings. Dashed expectations are admitted and quietly faced. A new set of expectations slips into place.

As family members work through their own

reactions, at least some of them will no longer perceive the stressor as being a crisis. These relatives can then provide some of the emotional support the young person, who is dealing with a critical sexual or lifestyle choice, needs. In doing this, parents and relatives should keep certain factors in mind.

Changing Standards

Today's young adults are more open about their sexual activities. More liberal standards for sexual behavior have encouraged greater sexual activity. Young Americans began to accept sexual permissiveness and public display in the 1960s; in the 1980s, the pendulum has swung back. In earlier decades children engaged in sex play and continued it into their teens. Since sex and marriage were for procreation, religious and societal teachings placed the label of "sin" on premarital sex. It was hidden. Today, however, marriage no longer has a primary purpose of procreation: it is two individuals publicly acknowledging their long-term commitment to each other.

Children begin their sexual lives—physically, hormonally, and emotionally—during the teenage years. In general, teens express the same concerns and desires expressed by earlier generations. Sometimes they hide preadolescent sex play, but are more likely to be open about their private choices.

However, even teenagers who have good communication with their parents may keep some of their sexual activities hidden. But when major difficulties arise, the teen usually turns to parents. If and when this happens, parents should open the doors of communication.

Active Sexuality and Parents

Acting-out teens are trying to establish the parameters of a satisfying sexual life. Often the young adolescent boy is worried about what turns girls on, whether boys are more interested in sex than girls, and what emotions characterize female behavior. The adolescent girl has similar concerns about boys.

Both boys and girls vaguely recognize that pregnancy is a possibility, but many assume their partners will be responsible for preventing pregnancy. In fact, fewer than half of the adolescent males who are sexually active are using contraception regularly. Most boys and girls count on luck. Some males assume the female will protect herself, while females assume the opposite. Some do not want to be embarrassed by the awkwardness of using a condom or diaphragm. Still others practice coitus interruptus. Parents should help their children to understand, through on-going communication and sex education, that one of the real tests of maturity is becoming a sexually responsible adult. Pregnancy information as well as information regarding protection from veneral disease, herpes, and AIDS are needed in our society.

Parents who do not insist that their teenagers use contraception, or who keep quiet about contraception, reason that they do not wish to be the cause of their child indulging in sexual activities and, unknowingly, contribute to the problem. Parents should talk with their maturing children about the use of contraception: they should explain that it is a normal practice, and that care and respect for self and others is incumbent in sexuality. They should emphasize that both parties have equal responsibility for their sexual relationship. Many girls avoid planning ahead, because they feel it would take the romance out of love happening naturally. They are more likely to ask relatives or friends than parents to get them the pill. Boys are often too embarrassed to purchase condoms. However, little clues and hints are often used to test the waters with parents. Young adult children begin to ask questions or talk about the sexual activities of their peers and, if communication is good, the time may arise for one of those teachable moments. The subject of contraception can, of course, be discussed during the pre-adolescent stage and mentioned now and again in the following years. Discussions about sexual feelings and practices, if they are open and shared, will strengthen family bonds.

POSSLQ

The United States Bureau of the Census developed a new acronym for Persons of Opposite Sex Sharing Living Quarters: POSSLQ. Advice columnists, such as Ann Landers and Abby Van Buren, publish letters from parents asking how to introduce their children's live-in partners.

Investigators publish articles describing the satisfaction with marriage of former live-in partners with the marriages of those who did not cohabitate. Some courts have held that assets of cohabiters are community property to be equally shared. Cohabitation has become part of the American scene.

What differs from what our grandparents called "shacking up" is that the partners today are quite open about their living arrangements. It is not common-law marriage because the partners proclaim that they are *not* married. They are not promiscuous, although either may occasionally have other sexual partners. The general tenor of the relationship is that of commitment. The couple usually assumes traditional husband-wife roles. They believe they are in love.

In those relationships that have lasted six months or more, many partners feel they are testing their compatibility. They share goals and chores as though they are married. They reduce the chance of disease and sexual exploitation. Moreover, young men and women have discovered that random sex is exhausting and lacks romance and purposefulness and thus seek long-term commitment.

PARENTAL CONSIDERATIONS

Faced with these open revelations regarding their children's sexual choices, parents today are forced into sorting out their own reactions. They cannot ignore what is going on, because today's young adults are not willing to be secretive about it. Young couples show up at family functions together and expect to be treated as young marrieds.

Once they get over the initial nervousness, parents discover that one aspect of the POSSLQ relationship is that everyday concerns and problems of the young adults' household place their sexual relationship into a minor role. That the couple is expressing intimacy within the context of a commitment to each other's welfare makes it more acceptable.

Since it is unclear from existing data whether

living together encourages greater happiness after marriage, parents can only hope for the best. After all, the young adult presumably has been raised with certain assumptions about being treated respectfully and treating others respectfully. Parents have to trust that their child shows good judgment toward developing a positive relationship, and that this goal will guide them.

Parents do have to decide how to handle some issues, such as logistics in their own homes and in social gatherings. Will the couple be housed together when they stay in the parental home? Are younger, impressionable children present in the household? If so, what will be the effect on them when the couple sleeps together in the home? How will the couple be introduced? Parents should discuss these problems with each other and agree on some ground rules which suit their lifestyle. Then they can discuss these rules with their adult children in a non-threatening way. Discussing a current movie or television show which illustrates sexual styles gives parents the opportunity to make their ideas clear and to express their own values without condemning those of their adult children. Parents have the right to uphold their own standards of behavior in their own houses. Nevertheless, once the adult child lives outside the family domain, parents can no longer mandate the child's sexual behavior or choice. But they *can* encourage responsibility and non-exploitative behavior in their adult children by continued open communication of their own and other's values, and by helping the child to see him- or herself as an intrinsically good and responsible individual.

The couple ordinarily wants to maintain good

relationships with parents and siblings. But most will continue to live together despite parents' withholding of emotional support. When parents do not like the chosen partner, the reactions will create the same type of strain as that found in situations where a son- or daughter-in-law is not liked. The strain breaks up some marriages. In others, the couple simply removes the strain by severing their relationship with disapproving parents. The question is: If parents disapprove of their child's partner, should that disapproval sever the supportive link to their own child? If parents correctly foresee disaster, certainly the adult child is going to need them, and if the relationship prospers, the bonds between parent and child will be forever damaged.

If disapproval of the arrangement is paramount, the parents can either hide disapproval, or make little effort to conceal it and make interaction uncomfortable. Discomfort, however, need not completely eliminate communication.

In the first tentative discussion between parents and young adults about a living-together situation, the young adult usually reassures the parents: It is love. It was not a hasty decision. The commitment is there.

When quarrels send the young adult fleeing home, the parents must be as careful as they would about giving advice in a quarrel between a married couple. The couple has to work things out themselves.

Throughout the period of the relationship, parents can share their observations, discuss experiences with problem solving, help the young adult adjust, and trust that upbringing taught a good sense of values. And keep in mind that a commitment to another human being enhances one's own growth.

CONCERNS ABOUT HOMOSEXUALITY

As teens grow up, they reveal how they have accepted their gender role, gender identity, and sexual orientation (i.e., erotic preference). One's role and identity as male or female are realized in adolescence. Sexual orientation may or may not be revealed openly. Much homosexual activity in adolescent boys has a strong heterosexual flavor. It is usually a preliminary exercise to the behaviors that will be tried with the opposite sex later on and is often outgrown by adulthood. Heterosexual boys integrate their sensual experiences with attraction to the opposite sex. If your teenaged or young adult child seems confused about his or her sexual identity, counseling with a professional may be a step you want to suggest tactfully.

However, some young men and women do not integrate their adolescent same-sex experiences with opposite-sex attraction. For them, a continuing same-sex attraction may be suppressed for several years. The suppression occurs because family and society do not countenance same-sex attraction. Historically, between four and ten percent of adult males have had an erotic preference for the same sex. However, only a small percentage is exclusively homosexual. The percentage of homosexual women is less than half that of males.

When the young homosexual decides to live a homosexual lifestyle, his or her "coming out" is akin to the adolescent sexual phenomenon that accompanies identity formation. Only by acknowledging acceptance of oneself as a homosexual does one become, in the eyes of the homosexual community, gay. "Gay" implies acceptance of self and a transformation in one's views as well as a re-evaluation of previous experiences as positive. The major difference in the gay sexual orientation is that the greatest support comes from within the gay community rather than society at large.

Once a young adult has made the decision to live as a homosexual, parental acceptance of that choice is important. The parent *can* accept both the child and his or her choice of lifestyle as a valid one without being happy with, or approving of, that choice. And that acceptance is necessary if the two generations are to maintain a relationship.

Together with homosexual couples, bi-racial couples have to face the stress of minority status. In the bi-racial couple, one person has already learned how to tolerate the status. When a couple is both bi-racial and same-sex, the difficulties of confronting prejudice are compounded.

Families can help by talking over future problems with the couple. By helping the couple learn roles before the role is needed, learn how to compensate for vulnerable areas, and learn to transfer previous successful experience with stressors to the present situation, parents can lend emotional support to their adult children.

Much depends upon the couple's inner strength. Strength is built upon a strong self-concept and previous experience with successfully handling stress. Strength also depends upon the support systems available to a person and the quality of the couple's relationship. Resourceful families will undergo a reorganization of attitudes and be able to successfully interact and extend the quality of their relationships. A couple with a strong relationship may move beyond stress to attain a sense of stability. The movement is possible when decision making is shared, non-verbal and verbal communication regarding old norms, biases, and superiority/inferiority issues are discussed, and new standards are substituted and followed.

UNWED PARENTS

Over one million teenagers became pregnant last year and this statistic is rising. The sheer numbers of teen pregnancies suggests that parents need to be more open in discussing matters of contraception, the choices available, and the responsibilities of sexual behavior.

When parents learn that their own child is pregnant or has fathered a child, they feel shocked, angry, and frustrated. These emotions are often followed by self-recrimination: What did I do wrong? What will the neighbors think? What will I tell the rest of the family? The difficulty of handling their own inner conflicts impedes parents in giving their children the support they so desperately need. Yet it is crucial that *both* parents and child marshal their inner reserves and concentrate on finding a solution rather than on passing judgment.

Each parent, the girl, and the baby's father (if he is willing and able to take on the responsibilities) should have a voice in the final decision. Feelings and consequences should be explored and weighed. Parents should give their child as much emotional support as they can without promising more than they are willing and able to do. Overprotection can be as damaging as withdrawing support. It is best for child and parent to be honest and candid with each other so that realistic choices can be made.

What are the options available to unwed teenage parents today?

Marriages: Marriages between teenagers often end in divorce because of the complexities of problems which beset them. Therefore, those teenagers who choose to marry should explore with their parents and a counselor, if possible, their financial, educational, and emotional goals and be totally honest with one another about them.

Adoption. Giving up a child or a prospective grandchild is a painful decision but, in many cases, a beneficial and positive one. Few teenagers are able to be completely self-supporting, much less take on the care of another person. Parents can explore adoption possibilities with their child, but should not dictate that their adult child relinquish the baby. However, parents must be candid in setting limits as to how much and what kind of support they will give.

Abortion. Abortion is a legal alternative today. Discussion of the adult child's feelings and the parents' feelings about such a procedure and its long-term and short-term physical, moral, and emotional consequences is essential. Professional counseling on the physical and psychological risks, procedures, and costs of abortion can help your child make her decision with, if possible, the support of her sexual partner.

Single Parenting. Teenagers as well as more mature young adults who choose to have a baby without being married are no longer rare. Yet to parents who were raised in a time when marriage was considered a prerequisite to parenting, their unwed child's choice may seem scandalous. Parents who are faced with this circumstance and are unable to adjust to it should seek professional counseling, since the ultimate question is not whether they approve of unwed parenting, but whether they want to maintain a relationship with their child and grandchild—and how best to accomplish this objective.

CHILDLESSNESS

In earlier eras children were thought to be a natural and necessary concomitant of every marriage. Childlessness was looked upon as a great misfortune. Today, however, some couples do not choose to have children, much to many parents' dismay. However, not every young adult wants to or would be able to make a good parent. Exploration and discussion of ideas on this subject between generations can clarify each person's attitude, but the final decision to have or not have children is not one grandparents can make.

Today's sexual and social life-styles can be very different from the traditional ones embraced by past generations. Nevertheless, we must all accord to one another the freedom to live with dignity in our own ways. As parents we can share, explore, and discuss our values with our adult children, but the final choice as to the rules they live by is theirs.

CHAPTER THIRTEEN

HELPING YOUR CHILDREN GROW THROUGH DIVORCE

"We thought our daughter Barbara was in a dream marriage to a wonderful doctor. It was a shattering blow to have her call up and inform us she had filed for divorce. It was the usual case of the wife being the last to know he was unfaithful. With all the lawyers settling things, she goes from numb to angry and dumps her worries in our laps. And, too, we fear for what that anger is doing to our grandchildren," said stocky, balding Mr. Blackhawk. "Now my son-in-law promptly moved in with his girlfriend."

"My daughter's been divorced three times. My granddaughter has had four different fathers. Her mother insists the kid needs a father. Talk about worried." Silver-haired, ruddy Mr. Steen threw down his golf bag. "My granddaughter is entangled in 'his, mine, and ours' nightmare of stepbrothers and stepsisters."

The breakup of a marriage, like the breakup of a ship, plunges the people involved into unfamiliar depths and sends out ripples and reverberations that disturb the most serene family pool of relationships. But the fact is that today unhappy spouses no longer stay in situations that wreck their psychological growth potential.

The main reasons for divorce are still alcoholism, infidelity, and incompatibility. The divorce rate has spiralled because, in the opinions of young adults, many of the old admonishments turned out to be faulty. Among them:

"You must stay together for the sake of the children."

"Any *adult* can work things out."

"Divorce destroys the family."

Belief in these faulty assumptions meant that children were often kept in a household with poor adult models, suppressed anger, and stress. Most of the time the mother was assumed to be a dependent, childlike creature instead of an adult. The father was expected to protect, support, achieve, and always be wise.

By the time a person suing for divorce has become indifferent to the marriage and has exhibited psychological growth as shown in Figure 13–1(a), the stresses on the rest of the family are less intense than if the divorce involves continuing anger or recrimination, longing, or feelings of betrayal or rejection, as shown in (b).

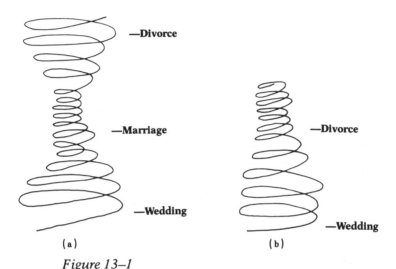

Figure 13–1
Spiral (a) indicates the hope and expectations on the wedding day replaced with constricted growth due to incompatibility during years of marriage, until the partner experiences psychological growth and the strength to divorce. (b) illustrates the divorce occurring suddenly and the intense emotional constriction that follows.

How children are affected depends in great part upon their ages. How the ex-spouses interact with each other and their children depends upon psychological strength and maturity. In-laws are usually expected to take the side of their own children as the wronged party.

Certain emotions and problems can be expected to surface in the aftermath. Parents can assist their children in accepting and exploring these feelings and issues.

The bewilderment expressed by the Holts in Chapter Three, and by Mr. Blackhawk and Mr. Steen in this chapter, reflects the pressures their assumptions and experiences about the stability of marriage undergo when children's marriages break up. They themselves had believed in marriage and society's admonishments about divorce and worked through problems as society said they should. Consider the older generations' lifetimes (Table 1–2). They were hard-working, family-centered husbands and fathers; war and other worldwide events had affected them personally but most of them had believed in society's traditional values. Now, they must admit that the roles they modelled for their daughters and sons were probably not effective. And because the parents' marital experiences are very different from their children's, the parents have difficulty in helping their children cope. Yet, despite generational differences in values, parents can provide understanding and help.

Transition after the loss of a relationship evokes certain emotions. By helping the young adult anticipate these emotions and acknowledge them, parents can encourage their children's psychological growth during and after a time of stress. Grandchildren's adjustment can also be encouraged and facilitated in the same manner.

The transition to being single and a single parent also generates problems that must be solved. These problems may be inextricably intertwined with emotions, may be situations that were formerly handled within the normal ebb and flow of parental and spousal duties, or may be peculiar to the new

single status. Parents may need to help the divorcing
adult child overcome lack of skills or information.

TYPICAL EMOTIONS AND PROBLEMS

Emotions vary in intensity, whether one can
anticipate having the emotion or not. However, anticipation that a particular emotion may occur makes
it easier to disclose feelings. Typical emotions that
follow the loss of a relationship include confusion,
euphoria over being free, vacillation, anger, guilt and
projection of guilt, bleakness, fear, and tension.

Confusion. The loss of a partner through divorce means that a dramatic shift occurs in a person's
view of self-as-okay and of life as an orderly, predictable process. Sometimes the confusion causes people
to behave in ways incongruent with their usual character or to act in ways that are fraught with disorganized or desperate judgments.

Mr. Blackhawk's daughter was going through
periods of anger over being deceived, her good faith
having been taken advantage of, her picture of herself
as a loving wife and mother torn apart. She wondered, "Who am I?" This faulty self-concept was
tangled up with self-righteous retaliation at being
victimized, regret at the loss of prestige and status of
being married, and a desire to punish the perpetrator
in kind. Another example of a person who was confused was George Holt, in Chapter Three. He was
suddenly bereft of a partner who handled the kids
and household, and, also, he felt rejected.

Numbness is the flip side of anger. A person
can remain in a heightened state of anger only so

long. The times of examination, of reliving situational clues that were ignored, and of questioning the choice to divorce create a dizzy state (see Figure 13–1).

In the case of Barbara Blackhawk, angry interaction with her ex-husband is one way to keep some relationship going.

Some people reconcile several times because of confusion over the correct solution to relationship needs. Other people keep seeing each other privately and yet fight it out when their lawyers are present. Others may drive by the spouse's house or call them up all the time.

As the constant state of arousal and numbness continues, Barbara has trouble sleeping; she rearranges furniture in the middle of the night; she contemplates escape through suicide. These reactions convey her great sense of stress.

If her parents help her recognize that she has resources—in them, in her environment, and in the passage of time—she can acknowledge her hostile feelings. "I am angry. I am angry for a while and I seem numb for a while."

If her parents listen as she vents these feelings and, as time passes, help her let these feelings lessen and be replaced, she can begin a new life, gain a new reality, create a new view of herself.

"Who are you?" a parent might offer, "You are someone who, perhaps, will now reach her own potential. Let's look at your strengths and plan how you can meet change effectively."

Euphoria. Some people who have worked out their confusion describe a sense of relief at being free. They do not regret the loss of a relationship *per se,* because the love/hate attachment was so wearing and emotionally consuming that only indifference remained. While this euphoria often becomes tempered by reality, the person's psychological growth continues.

People who are glad to be free may, of course, also experience some other emotions now and then, but these do not often become debilitating. The energy that formerly went into the relationship becomes centered upon other people, such as children and those in the community, and on long-range plans.

If this temporary euphoria is dashed by other people, rejection, overwhelming problems, or thwarted plans, an understanding parent can step in with temporary relief or caring discussion of the issues involved.

Vacillation. Mr. Steen's daughter, indeed, does believe in marriage as opposed to meaningless sexual contacts, in being a homemaker for a husband who is a wage earner, in having a man be father to her daughter. She vacillates between some type of idealized view of marriage—probably because she perceived her parents' marriage as ideal—and her inability to recognize the needed commitment to work out problems that arise in intimate relationships. Moreover, she simply cannot identify those personal characteristics in men that complement her own and will help her achieve her high hopes for marriage.

Mr. Steen himself is having a difficult time coming to grips with his daughter's problem, as can be readily perceived through his conversation with Mr. Blackhawk:

> "First, Mary Beth married a guy who floated in and out of jobs, the house, and responsibili-

ties. As soon as she was pregnant, he drifted away permanently. I could understand that divorce. She even tried to trace him to offer a reconciliation. She had had enough experience fighting and making up with him by then that it seemed to her to be the only choice she had. We finally got her out of limbo, although I never thought I would advise divorce. But she was pretty and we told her she would find another man. She did. Mary Beth went to work in a bar—and my wife and I had never been in a bar in our lives—until she was too pregnant to work. After the baby daughter, Sue, came, she went back to the bar and married a guitar player. She left town with him and left the baby with us. Six months later she breezed home with a new guy, divorced the guitar player, and married this new guy.

"We were going crazy trying to talk some sense into her. When she was in high school, she was a cheerleader and we were so proud of her. There are still lots of nice young men she knew in high school that she could marry.

"Anyway, her next marriage lasted two years, during which time we neither had to care for her baby nor fear for what would happen next. So we could relax.

"Last year, it happened again. Mind you, I'm the one that keeps paying for the divorces. She came home, grumped around until I gave her the money for the divorce and then she took off for California with the baby . . . ripped the child away from us, you might say, when the little girl was only five years old.

"The first letter came three days ago saying

she married some Hollywood writer and is pregnant again. She said she hoped we were happy about the news. My wife and I are about convinced we should go to court to seek custody of Sue."

Mary Beth is fleeing the field rather than trying to endure her parents' disapprobation. She and her parents both want her to be happy. Unfortunately, her parents did not teach her how to weigh situations and try to anticipate consequences. This was because in the past the parents worked out their own problems with a combination of experience and knowledge of probabilities. Mary Beth was sheltered from such discussions.

Mary Beth tried to make her dreams of a happy marriage come true, choosing glamorous but weak males. She expected life to be like her dreams, a storybook life. When the pages of the storybook fell out, she was left with no other choice, as she read the scenario, than to write herself a new part, diametrically opposed to the one she had been playing.

She keeps returning to the childhood home and parental relationship, hoping Mommy and Daddy will kiss her wounds and make them well. However, this behavior pattern does not bring her the relief she seeks. She could be helped by discussion with her parents on future directions, what constitutes a good life, what ramifications of marriage relationships decisions must be weighed, and what ongoing tasks may arise.

Mary Beth does not understand herself and her own needs, much less those of the males in her life.

Although she wants and plays at motherhood,

perhaps meeting an unspoken belief that her parents will approve of her if she does, she appears to be heading into an unexpected confrontation with her parents over custody.

Her vacillation between being realistically married and demanding that certain romantic ideals of marriage be met, between being a responsible parent herself and fears of her ignorance of how one parents, between wanting her parents to care for her and being on her own, will require professional help. It has gone on too long and become a self-defeating pattern: a merry-go-round.

If Mary Beth's parents were more mature and had been able to communicate better with their child prior to her first marriage, they might have been able to provide some guidance on realistic marital expectations. However, the parents did the best they knew how; and guilt at this period will not help Mary Beth nor change the past.

Mary Beth still wants their love, still seeks approval. Her parents feel they express their support when they express concern for her child. Perhaps they do—perhaps not—but if they want to help Mary Beth they will have to do so in more direct ways: by exploring her feelings and helping her make better life choices.

Anger. Anger is a natural emotion that can be anticipated following a divorce. Although the legal system of divorce laws in some states has tried to reduce the acrimony that was implicit in identifying a plaintiff and a defendant by turning to no-fault terminology, people still expect that one party will be at fault. The two parties experience different reasons for their anger. On the one side may be sense of betrayal and rejection. Sometimes the feelings of betrayal and rejection are so extreme that a husband will terrorize his former wife and family. These same feelings may also take the form of hostile remarks such as, "I'm going to take that S.O.B. for every cent he has." Similar reasoning may ensue whether a person is the wronged or the right party since break-ups are seldom one-sided.

Barbara Blackhawk was angry because her trust in her husband had been betrayed and because she felt a sense of rejection as a woman. The latter feeling is complex and often accompanied by a sense of failure. "How could this be happening to me? I did everything the way it was supposed to be done."

Men, too, who have been in charge of their families, going to work every day to support them, buying them everything, are shocked when their wives leave them. They find the inexplicable desire to be rid of them on the part of their wives to be a label of failure.

A different solution may be perceived in a "friendly divorce." In such a case, no pervasive anger may arise, and the couple may be able to concentrate on joint parenting responsibilities and related obligations.

However, anger sometimes recurs at intervals after an amicable divorce. Like guilt, anger insistently returns because, although divorce is a voluntary choice and does not have the finality of death, there still remain unresolved feelings, often of a hostile nature.

By talking about and anticipating bouts of anger, parents can help young adult children plan to shift the energy generated by hostility into some work or other effort; of course, this can be attempted only after divulging the source of the energy. Even hostile energy can become useful and eventually dissipated within meaningful activities.

Guilt. Another major emotion parents can help grown children deal with while going through divorce is guilt. Some examples are: "What am I doing to the children? What could I have done differently? How did I get into this situation?" Parents can point out that often it is impossible to separate out exactly who is guilty of what aspect of the divorce—and above all it is useless to try and do so.

Quite often, however, it is useful to express feelings. As Barbara Blackhawk showed her anger, she recognized that part of it was due to feelings of guilt. This guilt reaction was also part of Mary Beth Steen's feeling that she somehow should have been able to create a responsible husband out of an irresponsible person. Becoming more realistic would better help Mary Beth to choose more appropriate goals and situations.

Blame. One of the difficult areas of guilt is the tendency to assign blame for what will happen to the children. A single parent formerly had a partner-in-power over the children and suddenly is alone. Two adults took care of the annual cyclical chores, or two adults contributed to upward mobility, and now the single parent or single household has been inundated with full responsibility. Each and every day there is a reminder of duties that it was the other spouse's responsibility to handle before the divorce took place. George Holt (Chapter Three) faced this problem.

Disorganization and despair can easily overwhelm divorced pesons who are faced with single parenting. They may simply give up, and blame any resultant disaster on the ex-spouse. They may make bad and quick decisions: relinquishing custody, giving up a good job and taking off for parts unknown, acting out in unusual ways, and generally showing poor judgment in their actions and decisions. Now and then these poor decisions are a form of self-imposed punishment, but usually they are merely impulsive decisions made at a time of discontinuity in their lives.

A parent can help grown children deal with guilt by helping them identify their desperate feelings or wishes to escape the emotional turmoil that goes on after a personal crisis affects a person's poor self-image. For others, the psychological growth that is possible when one is free to move ahead may be so intense that the person feels guilty over *not* feeling guilty. By noting that blame is seldom a one-way street and that outsiders' comments may be off target in expecting grief and self-blame to be the natural concomitants of divorce, parents may help their adult child recognize that there is nothing wrong with the feeling of elation, but that no one feels euphoria all the time. Often euphoria alternates with apprehension and anxiety, because no one stays high all the time and because all people, at times, feel confusion and depression.

Parents can help divorced children assume single parenting duties by pointing out that plans can be scheduled, time committed to those plans, certain bottom-line rules set up at home and, most importantly, that children must not become pawns of the bad guys versus the good guys. A single parent can be a good mother *or* a good father, and the opposite sex models can be generated from friends, family, and youth activities. Research indicates that a stable single parent is capable of providing quality time and secure attachment environments for his or her children.

Understanding family members can encourage single parents to feel competent and self-confident even in the face of outside criticism. Criticisms often fail to recognize the courage of the parent taking responsibility for the care and upbringing of the children. Critical statements from friends and relations rankle the insecure young adult. But parents might point out that someone can always be found who will criticize single parents for their children's overachievement, compulsive behavior, underachievement, mood swings, pleasant behavior, defensive posture, teenage interpersonal problems, and so forth. Moreover, divorce often causes financial and familial changes so that both guilt and outsider criticism further distress divorced parents who are told: A parent of a pre-school child should stay home; a parent should not be on welfare; no one should put their kids in child care; no single man can bring up a daughter who will be well adjusted; no single woman can bring up a son who is well adjusted; and so on.

Parents of grown children who are single parents can counteract their children's feelings of inferiority and insecurity by explaining in a complimentary and understanding manner that two-parent families are not a panacea for all problems in child rearing and one-parent families *can* successfully prosper.

Self-Denigration. Another area that generates guilt is the feeling that "some sin" led to the punishment of divorce. A concomitant rationale is that the young adult wrongly perceives that he or she should have been omniscient enough to forestall any difficulties. Parents can bolster the low self esteem that comes from such blame and help balance those negative emotions by contributing to their adult child's feelings of worth and their understanding of what can be controlled.

Pointing out resources in the environment that a young person can access and utilize may help overcome such feelings. Acceptance of the belief that "by the grace of God I can control and have the good sense to recognize that I can control" is important.

Parents should call frequently to chat and share memories of the child's trial-and-error successes and failures in other times and situations. The young adult needs to be reminded of the coping mechanisms he or she used in the past. A link with positive experience is a positive solution-rich tactic.

If despair is too deep-seated, the adult child should be encouraged to join a self-help group. Parent-to-Parent or Parents Without Partners and other groups for recently widowed or divorced people are located in most communities.

Bleakness. Once Mary Beth divorced her husband, she no longer fit in with the single life she knew in high school. Once the Blackhawk's daughter, Barbara divorced her husband, she no longer fit in with the couples in her social circuit. Moreover, neither one could afford to keep up financially with the single women they knew: Mary Beth because she had no income, and Barbara because she had no resources except those finances going to maintain the home for the children. So they were not only alone, but lonely.

Neither women had had a chance to develop good feelings about being single.

In both cases, the loss of the marital relationship—*not* the loss of the person they no longer loved and respected—led to a type of mourning. They had left a relationship of shared experiences, hopes, plans, and problem solving for that of being alone. They no longer had the familiarity of their house, of being coupled—with its ties and obligations—nor of mutual identification, no matter how faulty. They felt that their psychological growth would remain static forever.

Bleak feelings parallel intense regret over what might have been, the dream that was lost, the hopes that were dashed. Parents can help the grown child who feels depressed to overcome isolated and lonely feelings by suggesting activities, clubs, and interests so that the young adult can become involved in life again.

For the person who is close to being receptive and happy with being alone, the tasks are easier but still time-consuming. If they have already secured satisfactory work circumstances, what remains is to amend their social relationships, make new friends, or cultivate social relationships at work for an outlet. They have to discover which of their old friends remain. They have to deal with well-intentioned matchmakers. They have to remake their lives.

Parents can help the person who is wracked with loneliness overcome the fear of being lonely. This can be done by helping the young adult identify and then avoid, where possible, the situations that precipitate the emotion, and identify ways to distract him- or herself. Particular situations that seem to bring on loneliness *can* be anticipated and discussed. The lonely person may be overwhelmed by intolerable, unamenable feelings. This might be due to unreal assumptions about other people's relationships. Someone who only seems alive in a second person's aura needs to isolate characteristics of self-worth and strength. Lonely, divorced people may become desperate, clinging people. Such dependency prevents the forming of new relationships and a new lifestyle.

The desperately lonely person sometimes invents a rationale for returning to a hopeless marriage to stave off loneliness. Another strategy of loneliness is hounding the past spouse, or invoking evidence that the other party wishes to make up so that it seems that remarriage is a possibility, when this fantasy is in direct contradiction to reality.

Anxiety, tension, insomnia, restlessness, weeping, or overeating may be clues to the adult child's unstable emotional condition. Someone who seems to continually predict unrealistic outcomes for new relationships may be suffering from intense loneliness. Someone who makes romantic assumptions about what turns out to be a series of unsatisfactory relationships may be suffering from an inability to handle reality.

If parents decide that loneliness may be hindering their child's adjustment, they can begin some gentle challenging. It is not enough to diagnose a problem; the young adult man or woman must find meaningful solutions and outlets that are acceptable. With parental assistance, he or she can begin to have a positive regard for solitude. Reading a good book, listening to a good record, can be rewarding and enjoyable.

Parents should not give the impression that it is their wish for the divorced adult to start dating or find a new mate. If and when the person is comfortable enough to return to dating, the adult child will introduce the topic, indicating that a request for reactions is being made. At that time parents should offer positive and reassuring comments.

But premature pressuring by parents can be detrimental. A large percentage of divorced people remarry within three years. About a third of the second marriages among upper-class people end in a second divorce and a higher pecentage of middle- and lower-class marriages end the same way. Whether or not a second marriage succeeds, the continuing support and efforts by parents to help their adult children use a traumatic period as a period of personal psychological growth is essential. People who become comfortable enough with themselves to be alone but not lonely have achieved lasting benefits.

Fear. We read and see many stories of soldiers in fear for their lives, but no one reveals the fear of a suddenly single mother who is faced with ensuring survival for little children in a society which has not educated her for such a task, and doesn't provide her with child care facilities. No one has captured the fear of a suddenly single father faced with unexpected traps of sickness and daily care, of laundry, shopping, and cooking for his children, while making a living. No one has captured the heartsick fear of a woman who, married for twenty-five years taking care of children as well as husband, is suddenly deserted.

The soldier confronts a machine gun nest and risks his life. The divorced, single parent has to raise and guide children while confronting the uncertain fortune that threatens their lives.

The momentous decline in the economic status of most single mothers with children has resulted in a new poverty class. New laws that seek to collect child care payments are being passed. These laws were passed because only about a third of the child care awards made by courts are ever paid by fathers. Phyllis Chesler's book, *Mothers on Trial*, chronicles how fights for custody place women on trial and how males brainwash children and terrorize former wives to win settlements. In her study, two-thirds of the fathers who sued for child custody did so for economic reasons—in order to keep the house, avoid alimony and child support payments.

Data reveal that the households headed by single females take a sudden drop in economic status following a divorce, while the disposable income of the single father, who ordinarily does not receive custody of the children, rises. Single mothers should learn to be assertive, review how to deal with agencies, and develop the facility to interpret legislation. These skills can provide respite from nonproductive emotional states.

Tension. All of the aforementioned emotions can foster tension, create stress in interpersonal relationships, and lead to incapacitating active responses. Tension can lead to the "overs:" overeating, overdrinking, overworking, over-risk-taking—such as driving too fast or adapting promiscuous lifestyles. Parents can be alert to nervous mannerisms and speech patterns that are not typical of the person;

these may signal tension. Often, the tense person seems unable to sit still and has trouble sleeping.

When parents recognize the signs of acute tension, they can help their disturbed grown children to ease the situation. Acceptable outlets for tension can be gauged once a young person has been helped to recognize and acknowledge the signals. For example, a parent may be yelling at the children all the time and then hugging them. That person needs some respite from the kids, as well as a personal healing activity. By providing short-term babysitting services, giving the tense young parent a few hours of private time, older parents can help their adult children learn to cope.

A general formula for parents to apply in helping their grown children through the first year following the divorce is (a) help them anticipate their emotions; (b) encourage them to acknowledge their emotions ("You have a RIGHT to be depressed"), and explore possible reasons for depression, thereby lowering the devastating effects and enabling them to let the feelings run free; (c) help them examine and adjust to their new reality; (d) assist them in discovering and using resources such as people, agencies, things; and (e) help them identify previous experiences in decision making that included problem definition, alternative sorting, and action.

In reality, there is no single solution to effectively handling the trauma of divorce. But parents can express to their adult children that there is opportunity for those who are willing to work through their problems to experience extensive psychological growth and to create a new and often better life.

CHAPTER FOURTEEN

THEY NEED TO GET A JOB

Mr. Ramirez spoke softly. "They have trouble getting and keeping jobs. Until they learn how to knuckle down, I doubt things will change. They need to get a job and stick with it. Am I going to support them all my life?"

Mrs. Williams added sadly, "I share your concern. My daughter has reading and learning problems. I'm afraid she won't even try to be independent and then what will happen to her when Bill and I die?"

Mr. Kopetchez commented, "My son came home from the Vietnam War. All his buddies were well into their careers. He says he felt he needed to do his bit for his country and is not bitter that no one hires him in a permanent position. But it's been ten years."

"My daughter, Julie, just got out of college; she moved back into our home and doesn't seem to be able to find a job." Mr. Robinson shook his head resignedly.

Today's job market is very different from those of the past. Parents are from an era in which one assumed a natural progression from education to work; many feel bewildered themselves about the intimidating parade of new technological job titles and functions. Young adults are equally bewildered; often they are left behind before they can begin.

As discussed in Chapter Four, a lack of motivation to work on the part of the adult child may also be operating. This deficit is characterized by lack of awareness, lackadaisical attitudes, insecurity, and disrespect. For some young people, not working is more rewarding than working.

Others, who want to work—such as Mr. Kopetchez's son and Barbara Blackhawk (Chapter Thirteen)—missed a traditional liaison stage between education and work.

Many young people feel threatened and so do not try to achieve success. The adult child who feels insecure clings to the nurturing cocoon of the home environment or feels betrayed by unrealized expectations (see Figure 14-1).

Young adults trying to enter the paid labor force have to learn strategies for job finding and to identify and market skills, and at the same time struggle with the emotional issues surrounding their situation. Parents can affirm the job seeker's hopes for success and provide information on job-seeking and self-marketing strategies. This help involves an objective examination of interests and abilities, possible testing for aptitudes and interests, and practice in being interviewed. Maturing adults need support in their beginning stages of deciding upon and obtaining a vocation. It is a threatening time, and the threats seem to take many forms and produce certain observable reactions.

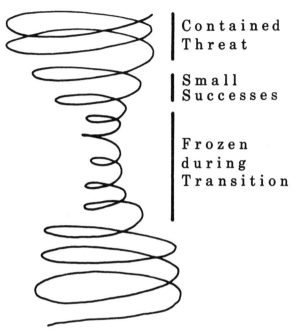

Contained
Threat

Small
Successes

Frozen
during
Transition

Figure 14-1
Those who feel threatened do not seek appropriate employ-
ment and so their personal growth is frozen until they learn to
deal with their fears and insecurities and to move from
"fearful child" status to "creative adult" status.

EMOTIONAL COMPONENT

High school and home life are safe, secure
environments. A person may not have consciously
observed a model or mentor making the transition to
work. The appropriate steps and behaviors are not
explicit. The person may feel threatened and, therefore, fear that he or she will fail. The person may feel
insecure about the identity he or she has held in
family and society. Financial burdens appear overwhelming.

As a result, many young people's insecure feelings about themselves are compounded by low aspiration levels, fear of failure, role conflict, perceived consequences of becoming achievement-oriented, and lack of assertiveness skills.

These threats can be reduced by small successes, positive consequences, positive information, and exposure to models. As the person gains control over the situation, his or her psychological well-being increases (see Figure 14-1).

PHYSIOLOGICAL REACTIONS

Threats can also result in physiological symptoms. Psychiatrist Thomas H. Holmes developed a stress scale based upon positive and negative major events in a person's life (see Chapter Fifteen). The stress scale indicates that eighty percent of the people with over three hundred stress points within one year may have serious illness within two years, versus thirty-seven percent of the population with one hundred fifty points or less. Changing jobs, including going from non-paid to salaried work, is worth thirty-six points; divorce, seventy-three points; fired from work, forty-seven points; business re-adjustment, thirty-nine points; change in financial status, thirty-eight points; change in work responsibilities, twenty-nine points. Obviously, many little experiences culminate in these large-scale fears.

Positive Use of Fear. People who are able to channel fear become more purposeful. Parents can help by expressing belief in the young person's abilities to cope. They can help the person find aptitude testing bureaus and they can help the individual rehearse interview behaviors. They can share experiences and identify strategies useful by successful models without, of course, comparing the adult child unfavorably to the model. Parents and grown children should be aware that some measure of anxiety is good, because it energizes the person. Fears *will* recede when a job is found.

JOB FINDING

Merely exchanging unpaid work experience for *any* job is a poor bargain. Parents and children can discuss the work ethic, and parents can stress that a job should give satisfaction as well as a paycheck. Often young people need money, but when a paycheck is the sole concern, they may not take time to identify and use their talents and skills. They may live in small communities where there is little opportunity and they may fear moving. They may want to be finished with seeking jobs. So, what is actually emphasized in the method of job seeking may be influenced by the values held. Sometimes short-term solutions may be more important than satisfaction, training opportunities, stability, or advancement opportunities. However, when a young person seeks a career, long-term solutions should be found.

Procedures. Novice job seekers have two methods available to them in a job search. Informal methods are directly applying to prospective employers and asking friends, relatives, or teachers. Formal methods involve applying through institutional intermediaries such as the state employment service, private employment agencies, school placement officers, labor union hiring halls, and advertisements in

newspapers or journals. Advertisements are classified as formal from the job seeker's point of view
since employers by placing ads offer a number of
opportunities from one source of information with
low cost to many applicants in money and time.

In a tight labor market, employers may increase their reliance on newspaper advertisements
and other formal methods to get the widest possible
exposure to their job openings. The Department of
Labor research staff wrote:

> Formal methods can offer the greatest amount
> of information about job opportunities in gen-
> eral, but may not yield much specific informa-
> tion about each job opening. On the other
> hand, informal sources of job leads, such as
> friends and relatives, may be able to provide
> more extensive or detailed information with
> respect to fringe benefits, prospects for promo-
> tion, working conditions, and training oppor-
> tunities. In searching for job information,
> workers are faced with an optimization prob-
> lem: they must balance the potential benefit of
> additional information against the costs in-
> curred in obtaining it. . . . In a tight labor
> market, for example, young workers might
> depend more on informal "grapevine" search
> methods. During periods of high unemploy-
> ment, some may prefer to use more formal
> methods, such as private employment agen-
> cies, since the return may justify any fees paid.

The Most-Used Strategies. In the early 1970s the
United States Department of Labor surveyed sixteen
million employed wage and salary workers sixteen

years old and over who were not in school and had started a current job in 1972, when the unemployment rate was between five and six percent. About one third (5.5 million) of these workers had not actually looked for work because they (a) returned to jobs formerly held, (b) were offered jobs, or (c) entered a family business. About half of the remaining 10.4 million job finders were new entrants or re-entrants to the labor force. The other half had quit jobs or lost them.

Major findings pointed out the most used methods and also provided a list of methods that were not chosen very often.

Two out of three job seekers, of both sexes, applied directly to employers without suggestions or referrals by anyone. Incidentally, this held true for people from small towns as well as those from large Standard Metropolitan Statistical Areas, both inner city and outer city.

The next five methods used most frequently were: (1) asking friends about available jobs at their places of work, (2) answering local newspaper ads (these two were used by only ten percent of the workers in small towns, compared with over forty percent using direct application), (3) asking friends about jobs at places other than where they work, (4) checking with the state employment service, and (5) asking relatives for leads.

Men tended to use an average of 4.2 methods and women, fewer at 3.7. However, partly because they found a job sooner, women who devoted full time to their families before searching for a job used an average of 2.8 methods, compared with 4.4 methods for women who had lost their existing jobs.

Perhaps this difference occurred because women newly entering the work force settled for less: low paying jobs doing anything.

Blue-collar workers tended to ask friends second most often, after applying directly. White-collar workers tended to answer newspaper ads next most often after applying directly.

How well do these methods of job seeking work? Thirty-five percent of workers obtained jobs through direct application to employers and twelve percent each by asking friends about jobs where they work and by answering local newspaper ads. About five to six percent of the job seekers obtained jobs through private employers or the state employment service. The United States employment service, Job Service, offices serve every county in the United States. Employment and Immigration offices function throughout Canada, and their services are free. About twenty percent of all job openings are handled by Job Service. Special interviews and counselors at Job Service work with handicapped persons and veterans. Job Service also offers counseling, aptitude testing, and a computerized job bank.

About half of all persons who applied directly to employers found jobs. This is about double the percentage for the methods with the next two highest rates.

The majority of job hunters found jobs within four weeks, although relatively fewer men than women found jobs in that period of time.

The duration of the job search was generally about the same regardless of the method used. However, for each individual job seeker in a given economic climate, finding a job quickly depends more on factors such as wage expectations, geographic location, experience and skills, motivation, and financial resources than on methods used.

One out of three job seekers turned down an offer. For about a third of these, the job was rejected because of the location, hours, or other unsatisfactory working conditions. Obviously, people who use several methods of job selection have more choices available.

Discussing these practical techniques with your inexperienced or insecure young job seeker may provide needed information about the "hows" of finding a satisfying, secure lifestyle. Many young adults retreat from the work world, not out of laziness but of fear that they are inadequate to compete. Practical answers and techniques explored and discussed between parent and adult child—without the parent usurping control—are very good ways of focusing the young person's attention upon reasonable, available choices and of helping to narrow those choices down to constructive job-seeking strategies.

For young people, the most fearsome aspect of suddenly trying to move into salaried employment is understanding exactly how their years of schooling and prior experience translate into marketable skills. This translation was briefly mentioned in Chapter Four. Youthful job seekers have to understand the structure of the work world as well as how their own interests and competencies mesh with that structure. Parents can help their adult children and assist them in preparing to be a part of that world by finding out and discussing different available techniques for assessing career interests and aptitudes.

One technique that has become popular is the

cluster concept, which furnishes some parameters within which one can work. As mentioned earlier, maturing adults can seek special assistance through Job Service. Vocational rehabilitation counselors can help handicapped young persons.

Older adults seldom have taken standardized tests such as an interest inventory, and tend to equate a notion such as *interests* with aptitudes. Interests are preferences or valued attributes. Aptitudes are competencies. Counseling grown children should probably begin with an exploration of their interests and competencies; these should be related to congruent work environments that satisfy the interests and require the competencies. Parents who want information regarding interests, competencies, and clusters should obtain the United States Department of Labor's *Guide for Occupational Exploration,* which is available at libraries.

YOUNG ADULTS' INTERESTS

Artistic: An interest in creative expression of feeling or ideas. The young adult who likes these activities can satisfy this interest in the creative performing arts or adjunct fields. He or she may enjoy literature, writing, or editing, and might consider newspaper or magazine publishing, advertising or teaching. He or she may prefer to work in the performing arts, directing, teaching, or performing in drama, music, or dance. He or she may enjoy the visual arts and could look into fields which have painting, sculpture or ceramics as a basis. Those who want to use their hands to create or decorate products could also search out careers as florists.

Scientific: An interest in discovering, collecting, and analyzing information about the natural world and applying scientific research findings to problems in medicine, the life sciences, and the natural sciences. Some of the ways a young adult can satisfy these interests are by working with the knowledge and processes of the sciences. He or she may enjoy researching and developing new knowledge in mathematics. Perhaps solving problems in the physical or life sciences would appeal. Some may wish to study medicine and help humans or animals. Any of the allied health careers such as nursing, dental technology, or health practice are good choices. Working with scientific equipment and procedures, for example, in research or testing laboratories, is a possibility.

Plants and Animals: An interest in activities to do with plants and animals, usually in an outdoor setting. Your maturing adult child can satisfy this interest cluster by working in farming, forestry, fishing, and related fields. He or she may like doing physical work outdoors, such as landscaping and gardening activities. Perhaps training or taking care of animals would appeal. He or she may have management abilities, which could be used in owning, operating, or managing farms, geological fields, such as parks, or other related businesses or services.

Protective: An interest in using authority to protect people and property. Young people can satisfy this interest by working in law enforcement, fire fighting, and related fields. They could investigate crimes or fires; they might prefer to fight fires and respond to other emergencies, or work in adjacent areas such as security. Perhaps a job in guarding or patrolling would be attractive. If they have management abilities, they could seek a leadership position in law enforcement and the protective services.

Mechanical: An interest in applying mechanical principles to practical situations using machines, hand tools, or techniques. These interests can be satisfied in a variety of jobs ranging from routine to complex. If the young person enjoys working with ideas about objects, a job in engineering or a related technical field can be attractive. Other fruitful areas for such interests are the crafts or trades, building, making or repairing objects. If the maturing adult likes to drive or operate vehicles and special equipment, he or she may prefer work in mining or construction.

Industrial: An interest in repetitive, concrete, organized activities in a factory setting. Such an interest can be fulfilled by working in one of myriad industries that manufacture goods on a mass production basis. The young adult may enjoy manual work—using his or her hands or hand tools. Perhaps they prefer to operate or take care of machines. They may like to inspect, sort, count, or weigh products.

Business Detail: An interest in organized, clearly defined activities requiring accuracy and attention to details, primarily in an office setting. Young people can satisfy this interest in a variety of jobs where they can attend to the details of a business operation. Some may enjoy using their math skills; a job in billing, computing, or financial record keeping would be satisfying. Others may prefer to deal with people and may want a job in which they meet the public, talk on the telephone, or supervise other workers. Personnel work would suit these skills. Those who like to operate computer terminals, typewriters, or bookkeeping machines can be helped to define their skills in terms of finding suitable equipment. Perhaps a job in record keeping, filing or recording would be fulfilling. Others may wish to use their training and experience to manage offices and supervise other workers.

Selling: An interest in bringing others to a point of view by personal persuasion, using sales and promotional techniques. The young job hunter can meet this interest in a variety of ways. Some may enjoy selling technical products or services; while some would prefer selling jobs requiring less background knowledge. There exist sales openings in stores, sales offices, or in customers' homes. Products may be bought or sold to make a profit. There are also sales-affiliated roles to play in legal work, business negotiations, and advertising.

Accommodating: An interest in catering to the wishes and needs of others, usually on a one-to-one basis. Young people who display enthusiasm for this type of service should look into the possibility of hospitality services in hotels, restaurants, airplanes, etc. Some may enjoy improving the appearances of others, as is found in the hair and beauty care field. Other possibilities are personal services such as travel agents, nursemaids, limousine services, taxi drivers, etc.

Humanitarian: An interest in helping individuals with their mental, spiritual, social, physical, or vocational concerns. There are many fields in which caring for the welfare of others is important. Perhaps the spiritual or mental well-being of others concerns the young adult: he could prepare for a job in religion or counseling. Some may wish to help others with physical problems: they could work in nursing, therapy, or rehabilitation fields. Others may like to provide needs by working as an aide, orderly, or technician.

Leading-Influencing: An interest in leading and influencing others by using high-level verbal or numerical abilities. Maturing young adults can satisfy this interest through study and work in a variety of professional fields. Some may enjoy the challenge and responsibility of leadership and could seek work in administration or management. Others may prefer working with technical details and, therefore, could find a job in finance, law, social research, or public relations. Others may like to help others learn. Perhaps the field of education would appeal to them.

Physical Performing: An interest in physical sports and activities. The young person with keen athletic prowess can gratify this interest through jobs in athletics, health and the fitness fields, coaching, teaching athletics, working in or owning a fitness center or spa. Jobs as ski instructors, swimming lifeguards, and sports coaches provide opportunities to make sports both enjoyable and profitable.

How does one determine a young adult's skills?

Measurement of competencies begins by looking at how the young adult deals with leadership, interpersonal social skills, motivation, written and oral communication skills, intellectual and judgment skills, and adapting and coping skills. The assessment is not necessarily dependent upon prior paid work experience, but upon competencies developed or used, for example, in school, volunteer work, extracurricular activities, leisure time, or daily chores.

DEVELOPING A PORTFOLIO

Parents can assist their adult children in compiling a portfolio which reflects competencies developed through experiences. It will be the basis for a *functional resume*. This differs from the traditional resume because it clusters competencies developed through volunteer and unpaid experiences rather than listing paid work experiences. A high level of specificity results from selecting experiences which demonstrate ability in tasks typically found in occupations.

For example, one young person may be helped to find themes in his or her experiences that demonstrate skills in Planning and Goal Setting, Organizational Management, Communication (Written and Oral), Decision Making, and Demonstrated Leadership Ability. In one research study, these particular skills formed "clusters" thought by experts to be required and marketable for the particular occupation of Educational Administration. The process of comparing one's competencies to job functions will probably enable broad application beyond one particular occupation.

Beyond identifying one's competencies to be clustered for a resume, developing a portfolio enables young people to perform more confidently in interviews. Interviewees are usually asked, "And just what can you do for this company?" Novice job seekers can answer that question specifically when they've gone through the process of documenting their own strengths.

Strengths also include good work habits. Meeting deadlines, being on time, low absenteeism, handling crises, and deporting oneself appropriately in class are good work habits. Parents can add much from their own memories of children's positive habits. This serves a two-fold purpose: it helps adult children recognize their strengths and it reinforces the idea that parent figures believe their maturing adult is competent.

In a traditional resume, the list of work experiences—that is, the job titles—imply certain related competencies. In a functional resume, experiences must be listed along with the functions that were performed in that experience. This will clarify the job-seeker's competencies and strong points. Then, they must be put together in an orderly format.

Normally, completion of the portfolio process takes approximately twenty hours. *The Quick Job-Hunting Map*, by Richard Bolles, available at many bookstores, can be used instead. The time taken to do the portfolio is well spent because the accumulated data is a valuable source of information for completing applications and resumes and preparing for interviews. And it is invaluable in helping the young adult gain control over threats to self esteem. Share the following with your young adult job seeker:

The first step is to record significant experiences which will provide opportunities to demonstrate necessary skills in your competency statements. List all

experiences, with the dates, that seem germane. This
will take some time. Include the dates on the left side
of this sheet.

*Second, think through the tasks, skills, func-
tions, or competencies* which were required in each
experience. A separate sheet of paper should be devoted to each Competency Profile for the selected life
experience.

*Third, select up to ten of these "job" experi-
ences* on the basis of whether they provided opportunities to demonstrate many competencies or an in-
depth skill in one competency area; whether they
represented a particular areas of competence otherwise not included; or whether they demonstrated a
skill beyond the area of specialization but of general
worthiness.

*Fourth, study the competency profile sheets that
display these selected experiences, then cluster related
competencies* under a descriptive title—such as Planning and Organization.

*Fifth, compose specific competency state-
ments from the variety of selected life experience under
each descriptive title* to reveal acquired skills to potential employers. The statements are worded to describe abilities under each title in the following style:

> *Supervisory Skills:* Developed and used per-
> sonal interaction techniques which minimized
> conflicts between paid and volunteer workers,
> decreasing the absence rate of the former and
> increasing the number and volume of pro-
> duced work by the latter (Red Cross Bloodmo-
> bile volunteer, 1977–78; Boy Scout Council
> member, 1981–85).

Sixth, carry the main headings and paragraphs over to a one-page resume. Center the individual's name at the top. Address and phone number are on the left, beginning on the next line. Then "Job Objective" is written as a one-sentence statement related to the entry-level job. This heading, and others, are set farther left than the information that follows each heading. Education is third. Competencies, or Work Experience, come fourth. Honors and Awards may be added here. Last are References, under which one can cite, "References Furnished Upon Request".

The final step is to help the young adult with the organization of the materials into a portfolio for easy retrieval. After pulling out the many experiences from memory, the cataloging of skills, the composition of descriptive titles and competency statements, and development of a functional resume with selected documentation, the final assembly is a rewarding experience. The file might include a cover page and table of contents. The material is thus available for revising the resume for another prospective job.

As with any important document, it is advisable to type the final copy.

JOB INTERVIEWS

Parents can rehearse interview questions and techniques with their grown children, and give them the advantage of practice.

Quite a bit of research has attempted to answer the questions of what constitutes interview behavior that wins one person a job over another person. The cumulative effects of going on a series of interviews and being serially rejected form a sense of defeat. A little warning flag goes up. The person begins to voice doubt. The United States Department of Labor calls the class of people who were at one time looking for work but no longer do so the *Discouraged Workers.* If discouragement occurs, role-play several interviews with your children. And review job interviewing techniques.

First of all, the young job seeker's best chance to make a good impression is through his or her resume. The resume may be the only picture the job seeker gets a chance to present.

When being interviewed in person, a pleasant smile, appropriate dress, good posture, and a firm handshake set the stage. Appropriate dress means wearing the clothes that are usually worn on that job. Appropriate dress also includes being clean and not smoking or chewing gum.

The second part of the impression is formed by one's verbal behavior during the interview. Being knowledgeable about the company, about one's own strengths ("This is what I can do for the company"), and about long-range plans is essential. The interviewer is not there to help a person discover how the job and person fit together; the job seeker must know what he or she can offer for the particular job.

Sometimes a job seeker will be sure that some questions that are asked are illegal. For example, no one can legally ask questions of a personal nature that solicit information not related to job performance. Interviewers from large companies are aware of this point; interviewers for smaller companies may not be, or may ignore the fine points of the anti-discrimination laws. Certain questions (marital status, number of dependents) that may *not* be asked in an interview must be asked, for income tax or health insurance purposes, after a person is hired. As Table 14–1 indicates, a person who suspects that illegal questions are being asked may or may not choose to prepare a reply.

Interviewers do not rate highly people who seem to want a job "for the experience"; the interviewer wants to hear that the job seeker will make a positive contribution for the company's—not the individual's—gain. Moreover, the resume may not have been read other than to check to see if some important clue is present. Some check only for the "knockout" factor—that one item that places the resume at the bottom of the pile: it may be that the job objective is inappropriate; that the printing is the wrong size; that the person wants too much or too little salary. These items may eliminate a person from consideration before *or* after the interview.

End the interview with a smile, expression of thanks, and a firm handshake. It is appropriate to write a thank-you note and to call or write later to inquire about the position's disposition.

Once the job search ends in success, one may well ask; is it a job or a vocation?

Spiritual, mental, and physical well-being should accompany the ritual of passage into the work world. The very word "vocation" means a "calling." One's internal voice says "this job, this position requires my particular attributes." The internal voice says "I am set apart by my unique fitness for the occupation." The voice says "a sense of duty is met by my presence."

Work is defined as application of energy to achieve a result. Results may not be those expected.

TABLE 14-1

SUGGESTIONS FOR FIELDING ILLEGAL
INTERVIEW QUESTIONS

- Laugh and don't answer.

- Chuckle and say, "You must be kidding."

- Keep the interview focused only on job specifications and job qualifications. Don't furnish information you don't want them to follow up on; do not give any opening by your own comments regarding spouse, kids, personal life. Be specific; generalities give them control.

- Do not assume that your personal and family lives *are* of interest or that these affect job performance. If you are a woman, consider whether the information would be volunteered by a man.

- Answer only those questions related to the job on the application blank; put a dash next to others. When they bring up the questions, you can say, for example, "I consider my marital status to be irrelevant."

- Be prepared to be honest about handicaps, but pair the information with a statement of how your willingness is enhanced or the handicap negated by other means.

- Placement or affirmative-action officers may be notified of infringements.

- Tactfully point out your understanding of the law and consequent impropriety of questions asked. "Is that relevant to this job?" might be gently asked after you've sized the questions up.

- Since questions that screen applicants in or out must be related to job success and therefore be data-based, show curiosity and say, "I myself have been studying how that (a person's age, plans for having children, etc.) affects job performance. Just what *do* your data show concerning the affects upon performance of workers here?"

- If you're slipped a question such as "Can you handle this?" or "Would your wife/husband approve?", simply be prepared to reply in a reassuring tone, "Oh, yes."

"Results," said Thomas Edison, "why man, I have gotten a lot of results. I know several thousand things that won't work."

Yet achieving results is reinforcing. The *calling* to continue performing to obtain results becomes a pleasant, exciting escalation of cause and effect.

Parents can explain to insecure young adult job seekers that there is a cycle of contribution and reinforcement which expands self respect. The satisfaction, in turn, increases.

The interest inventories cited in this chapter are based upon preferences of groups of people who are satisfied with their jobs, and have been satisfied workers for several years. The necessity of helping your young adult find that satisfied-good-worker combination is clear. Motivation and psychological growth potential are heavily imbued with individual proclivities toward personal self respect.

The very process of helping a grown child move into a vocation is an example of working toward a larger concern. The vocation of being a parent may have been thrust upon the parent, but human beings rise to the occasion. Their modelled behaviors teach the younger generation what can be gained by love, attention, and energy.

To encourage a young job seeker, parents' affirmation of the adult child as a valued person is important. With such support provided, the parents' suggestions regarding the several methods for job seeking will be much more effective. And once the small successes of each component are achieved, fears that prevent psychological growth can be overcome.

CHAPTER FIFTEEN

HANDLING JOB OR SCHOOL STRESS

"But there's another problem," said Mrs. Williams, her forehead creased in concentration, "Corrine won't work at all; Bill puts his work ahead of everything else . . . and then there's John. He is so crabby all the time, he snarls. His hands shake and he's always on edge. He's in sales and on commission."

"My daughter, Suzie, is going to college to be a teacher. She gets sick in the spring every semester right before exams. I keep telling her to take it easier, but she can't seem to pace herself," rejoined disgruntled Mr. Fattel.

Going to school is a pressured environment or becoming a worker in a highly competitive workplace often creates stress, and later, burnout, both of which constrict psychological growth. Unless one consciously works to prevent these outcomes and achieves a measure of equanimity, work or school becomes unproductive and unsatisfying. An individual—especially an insecure young adult—may be straining to grow, but instead becomes hindered by major stress or minor stresses.

Handling job or academic stress involves understanding the sources of stress and being willing to do something about those sources or about the reactions to the stress. We will look at the definitions and the costs of stress, sources of stress, and ways parents can help grown children handle stress.

What is "stress?" Being "under stress" is like "being in love": both are difficult to explain but easy to recognize when they happen to you. Pioneering professionals, such as Canada's Dr. Hans Selye in stress-effect research, Harvard's Dr. Herbert Benson in stress-reduction research, and Kansas State University's Dr. David Danskin in biofeedback techniques, tend to define stress through its physiological responses—particularly elevation in blood pressure, muscle tension, and gastrointestinal disturbances.

Selye describes how a person depletes psychic energy, which he terms *adaptation energy*, through constant reaction to unrelieved stress. Thresholds of tolerance to stress become lower and lower. Then minor stresses cause people to retreat, as in the cases of John Williams and Suzie Fattel-Brower, the two adult children cited at the beginning of this chapter.

When young individuals have great problems adjusting to the environment it may be described as stress reactions. Danskin points out that different individuals may manifest stress reactions in different systems of the body. One person shakes from muscle tension or has jaw aches from clenching his or her teeth. Another has migraines or dizzy spells. A third eats antacid tablets by the dozens.

An individual reacts to stressful situations because of the need of humans to protect themselves, which dates back to when primitive peoples had to be constantly on guard. Our bodies go into "guard gear" from a variety stresses. We all know that adrenalin floods the body during the stressful times and sometimes enables unusual feats of strength or daring. When a lower animal is aroused it will fight like a tiger or run like a jackrabbit. A human may lift a car or a tree to free someone.

The abilities of maturing adults to "go with the flow"—that is, to be flexible and feel in control of choices—is important. The differences in the *Type A*, hyperactive, time-pressured, coronary-prone individual and the *Type B*, flexible, related individual are examples of constricted versus flexible behavior patterns.

Human beings whose environments lead them to be excessively aroused readily manifest "flight-or-fight" responses in their bodily reactions. Often the environment does not permit them to effectively carry out required safety behaviors. As Danskin points out, primitive peoples had time to settle down between threats. Many young adults, confronted by multiple stresses, do not have similar periods of relief.

When a young person has just been severely criticized by his or her supervisor, teacher, or other authority figure, he or she will often react as though it were *destructive* criticism whether the criticisms were constructive or not. Indeed, receiving compliments from an authority figure can also be somewhat stress-inducing. Instinctively, those who feel threatened either fight or run away. But the correct learned behavior is to ignore instincts and listen. To do otherwise is not polite and mature, nor in one's best interests.

It is important for parents to keep in mind that stress, if not continual, can serve as a great stimulation for growth; when energy is not focused on survival, maturing adults can utilize it to expand their horizons.

Under stress, powerful hormones pour into the bloodstream and the nervous system prepares for immediate action. No matter what a person is consciously thinking, the nervous system is alerting organs and glands. Heart rate increases, perspiration pops out, hands feel clammy and the palms of the hands sweat *only* from stress or anxiety. When the bloodstream is rid of these energizing elements—for example, through vigorous exercise—the stress is no longer felt. When the employee or student sits there "taking it," the chemicals act continuously in a way that the system cannot tolerate forever without relief, and heart attacks or ulcers can occur.

Future generations viewing videotapes of present-day society's television commercials will be struck by the degree to which we are concerned with gamey armpits and gastrointestinal disturbances. Many billion-dollar businesses capitalize on our stress reactions.

Stress has been linked to other pathological symptoms and societal problems. These include hypertension, suicide, nervous disorders, allergies, asthma, insomnia, pill-popping, migraine headaches, marital discord, child abuse, spouse abuse, self abuse, lack of confidence, strike picketing, labor violence, alcoholism, depression, general anxiety, and a breakdown in normal relations with friends, family, and colleagues. Research coming from China even indicates that the intensity with which some people tried to solve the Rubik's Cube caused insomnia and high blood pressure. In addition to contributing to life-threatening diseases, stress depletes the body's energy and resistance levels, which results in exhaustion and burnout, which contribute to more colds and more flu. Young as well as older stressed people may turn to alcohol, smoking, over-eating, or drugs to try to keep the energy level up—or even to get a good night's rest.

From the physiological costs of stress we can project some of the costs to higher education and the workplace: absenteeism and turnover, increased use of personal leave and sick days, higher workman's compensation claims, more injuries, increased inefficiency. Moreover, productivity is directly disrupted by processes reflecting stress such as sourgrapes and complaints, and indirectly disrupted by fatigue and disease.

For example, one physician observed that during the spring she tended to be inundated with patients who were teachers in two disciplines: English and music. She found it no coincidence that senior class plays, high school productions, musicals and state music contests occur in the spring. As the stress levels grew, vague complaints became real pain and the teachers were struggling between commitments to their jobs and a crying need to stay home and find some respite from the competitive public performances of their students.

Since the 1930s and 1940s, when industry was first hit by an epidemic of executive deaths as a result of heart disease, the economic cost of stress has received increasing attention. The Aspen Institute for the Management of Stress estimates that premature death of employees costs American industry $25 billion per year. Industry spends money training executives and has so strong a vested interest in receiving a good return on that investment that more and more companies are paying for stress-management workshops and organized leisure activities.

Let's look at the sources of stress and some tactics parents can utilize in helping grown children avoid incapacitation. Stress sources include: one's own personal choices and structure of self esteem; the expectations of the system in regard to work or school; and factors in one's personal life that spill over into the workplace or classroom.

The structure of most young adults' self esteem is much less secure than it will be later in life. When a maturing adult's self esteem is perceived by him or her to be under attack, the body reacts to that stress by physiological changes such as higher blood pressure, racing heartbeat, and increased perspiration. Parents can be alert to these signs and aid their adult child in handling their feelings of stress.

Stress often also results from frustration when the attainment of a desired goal is blocked. When a maturing person has worked through the process of seeking a certain goal and finds a barrier, the barrier appears to be outside of one's control: the material for a report doesn't come on time; the promised check is not in the mail; the child's shoelace snaps just as his or her mother is ready to dash to the child care center; a tire goes flat in the garage, and so on. All of these external delays bring on failed promises or commitments that the person has made to himself, herself, or others.

Another condition of personal threat occurs from conflict, as when one is faced with a decision-making dilemma. Often the inability to make a decision is the result of several conflicting desires, and the inexperienced adult is unable to resolve the problem.

Each young adult brings personality characteristics to a job or school that flavor his or her experiences. Yet, there are expectations within the work system or classroom, as outlined in a job description or class syllabus, indicating that a certain level of performance is expected, regardless of who holds the job or enters the classroom. When the employee's or student's goals and the system's goals are congruent, the job or class is fun and rewarding. Of course even dedication can take its toll, as Bill Williams (Chapter Six) found out by being a workaholic, if one does not learn to stop and smell the roses along the way.

Sometimes a job or school stress also comes from elements in the work or school system that cannot be controlled. Favoritism, boredom, and no chance for advancement are three such sources. Another is promised recognition that turns sour. There is a shaggy dog story that illustrates this type of stress. A scientist, after working many years, finally constructed a clone of herself. The prestigious journals and newsletters reported this achievement and she got many requests to demonstrate the clone. Unfortunately, the clone had somehow developed a mind of its own and somewhere along the line learned all sorts of four-letter words and expressions about ancestry not fit for polite company and used them extensively when communicating. One morning when a group of renowned scientists were scheduled to visit the lab, the clone taunted the scientist with a string of very descriptive language pictures. The scientist became so angry that she pushed the clone out the window. Police came. They did not arrest the scientist for murder. The police arrested her for making an obscene clone fall.

If a job, especially at the beginning of a young person's career, does not provide a general sense of control over events and expectations, stress can take its toll. In a study of hospital and health records in Tennessee, it was found that the most stressful jobs were:

> Unskilled laborer
>
> Secretary
>
> Assembly-line inspector
>
> Clinical lab technician
>
> Office manager
>
> Foreman
>
> Manager/Administrator
>
> Waitress/Waiter
>
> Factory machine operator
>
> Farm worker
>
> Miner
>
> House painter

Stress factors most identified with these jobs included workload, deadlines, boredom, and responsibility. Blue-collar workers and white-collar clerical workers often have problems associated with depression, boredom, anomie, and sometimes alcohol or drug abuse. Withdrawal into being a workaholic or withdrawing from participation is a form of the "flight" response.

Burnout forms of the "flight" response occur in use of sarcasm, derogatory language toward a student, conflicts with other staff, being overinvolved in a problem, extreme competitiveness with others, and signs of fatigue. Problems with supervisors or teachers become manifest with feelings of harassment, of pressures, of hints to change assignments or simply of no support.

There is a curvilinear relationship between stress and work performance; too much or too little is debilitating; a middling amount is good. Supervisors and teachers, who themselves have a large load of stress from being responsible for others' performance, should be sensitive as to how they communicate the organization's or educational institution's expectations through their own communication skills, the definition of the work or pupil roles, the monitoring of these workloads, and the grasping of the overall impact of their own supervisory style upon their subordinates or students.

Drs. Holmes and Rahe several years ago developed a life stress scale isolating those life events rated highest by patients and relating the stresses to later illnesses. Through fifteen years of research, a definite relationship was found between ill health and discordant changes in one's life, that is, when the person perceived the life event as stressful. These findings are shown in Table 15-1.

TABLE 15-1
SOCIAL READJUSTMENT RATING SCALE

Event	Value	Your Score
Death of spouse	100	_____
Divorce	73	_____
Marital separation	65	_____
Jail term	63	_____
Death of close family member	63	_____
Personal injury or illness	53	_____
Marriage	50	_____
Fired from work	47	_____
Marital reconciliation	45	_____
Retirement	45	_____
Change in family member's health	44	_____
Pregnancy	40	_____
Sex difficulties	39	_____
Addition to family	39	_____
Business readjustment	39	_____
Change in financial status	38	_____
Death of close friend	37	_____
Change to different line of work	36	_____
Change in number of marital arguments	35	_____
Mortgage or loan over $10,000	31	_____
Foreclosure of mortgage or loan	30	_____
Change in work responsibilities	29	_____
Son or daughter leaving home	29	_____
Trouble with in-laws	29	_____
Outstanding personal achievement	28	_____

Event	Value	Your Score
Spouse begins or stops work	26	_____
Starting or finishing school	26	_____
Change in living conditions	25	_____
Revision of personal habits	24	_____
Trouble with boss	23	_____
Change in work hours, conditions	20	_____
Change in residence	20	_____
Change in schools	20	_____
Change in recreational habits	19	_____
Change in church activities	19	_____
Change in social activities	18	_____
Mortgage or loan under $10,000	17	_____
Change in sleeping habits	16	_____
Change in number of family gatherings	15	_____
Change in eating habits	15	_____
Vacation	13	_____
Christmas season	12	_____
Minor violation of the law	11	_____
Total		_____

With the permission of Microform International Marketing Corporation, exclusive copyright licensee of Pergamon Press Journal back titles.

As mentioned in Chapter Fourteen, eighty percent of the people who had a total score of over three hundred in a twelve-month period had a serious illness within the following two years. Note that the most points are for positive and negative personal crises; the first work-related item (fired from work) is in eighth place from the top in number of points assigned. This table can be used to help grown children explore and discuss the ways stress may be affecting their lives.

Because of this high cost of stress, many consultants and companies have come up with programs to help employees cope with stress. The programs are convenient and are reinforcing as they are being performed with colleagues. Educational institutions could improve the performance of students by adopting similar programs. Recently counselors and educators have begun to discuss the ways stress affects work and student performance. Some proposed solutions are:

1. Making mental health professionals available to employees, often called Employee Assistance Programs (EAPs);
2. Offering biofeedback training, teaching people to monitor and control physical reactions such as blood pressure, temperature (higher temperature equals a more relaxed state), muscle tension, and brain waves;
3. Bringing peers and family members together with students and employees to effectively discuss and restructure the environment during stressful times;

4. Offering nutritional examinations and dietary suggestions along with physical examinations;
5. Providing exercise lounges and physical fitness programs;
6. Scheduling daily time-out relaxation exercises;
7. Teaching students and employees how to "daydream" or use imagery, to call forth calming experiences.

What is stressful for one young adult may not be for another. What is relaxing for one person may not be for another. Once a maturing adult has comprehended and explored his or her physiological internal system of stress alarms, various tactics should be tried to help him or her achieve relief (see Table 15-2). Young people are often ignorant of or ignore body signals.

Initially, external clues may indicate stress, and parents can watch for these indicators in their adult children. Some of these are low morale, nervous behavior, absenteeism, job or school dissatisfaction, exhaustion, substance abuse, and sudden poor interpersonal relations.

What can be done?

Change of Pace. Since young people are not always able to find the kind of employment they want, some find their satisfactions and rewards outside of work, thus considering work as the means of paying for these outside activities. If the young adult's work is stressful or boring, some outside activities such as community work, hobbies, service, politics, religion, learning, or teaching can provide an essential change of pace until the adult child is able to reorganize his or her career goals and to find work which provides gratification.

Exercise and Diet. Most recreation and physical education programs now attempt to teach people lifelong sports: aerobics, tennis, swimming, golf, and racquetball. Sports are particularly relevant for active young people who reveal stress in muscular tension. A tactic for use at work is to tense the body, hold it, and release the tension suddenly. Or visualize gathering all tension into a closed fist and quickly release it. Isometric exercises also serve the same purpose.

Fortunately, we are experiencing a fitness surge and are curious about those components that go into a sense of well-being. Young adults today are into good health, including diet and exercise. Parents can sponsor or join their adult children in establishing new, healthier exercise and diet patterns. Diets replete with fresh foods, fish, and baked chicken provide essential minerals and vitamins, and exercise will produce greater energy and stamina.

Hobbies. Busy people have begun scheduling leisure-time activities for themselves, the same way appointments at work are scheduled. Hobbies cover the spectrum of human interests, but must be considered important enough to develop past the wish stage to the activity stage. Parents should explore and discuss grown children's hobbies, as well as careers, in an effort to make these activities a source of further rewards.

Relaxation and Biofeedback Techniques. A training program, book, or manual on relaxation techniques can teach the stressed young adult how to introduce systematic ways of inducing a relaxed state. Parents who use relaxation techniques might try doing one with their maturing adult. Start by saying: "Your feet are getting warm and heavy" and work up to actively relaxing other parts of the body. The listener should try to make him- or herself comfortable, with eyes closed, but not so comfortable as to drift off to sleep.

Biofeedback equipment consists of thermistors for recording temperature, machines to measure brain waves (the alpha state is similar to relaxation before going to sleep, and easily attained by creative personalities), forehead muscle tension, or heart rate. The physiological states of relaxation are taught so that people can control them without the machines, although brush-up sessions may be necessary. Many communities have biofeedback laboratories for this training.

Brainstorming. Teaching an adult child to talk out his or her needs with other people and brainstorm are extremely fruitful. Many ideas and strategies that have worked or been tried by other people as trial-and-error attempts to deal with stress can be adapted to one's own needs. Also, voicing one's concerns tends to put situations in a better light, rather than letting resentments ricochet around one's mind.

Worry. Advise an adult child that if a particular problem is worrisome, he or she should face that worry; either do something about it or find a means of achieving a balancing factor. A balancing factor offsets a weighty problem with a pleasant experience. If all else fails, then seeking professional help can reduce the perceived worrisome problem.

Degree of Involvement. Some jobs demand so

much emotional involvement from a person that the person feels like nothing but a shell at the end of the day. Discuss with your child the fact that caring people have a hard time leaving work at the office. One means of dealing with such stress that you might suggest is to shorten involvement time: devote periods of time to homework and reports, but schedule relaxation activities as well. Balance clients with committee work, allow for emergency needs of subordinates by shortening workloads, seek more help from the administration, take a vacation away from the phone.

Finding Control. Some things can be changed. Some things cannot be changed. Help grown children work on identifying what can be controlled or organized differently. Discuss accepting those things that cannot be controlled, going with the flow, and seeking other answers.

Humor. A sense of humor is extremely helpful and healthful. When item after item goes wrong while someone is doing his or her level best, the final horrendous straw—for instance, a flat tire—should elicit a laugh instead of tears or a broken camel's back. Teach your grown child to see the lighter side of his or her experiences by reviewing them together.

Delegate. Young competent people often want so much to succeed they sometimes get overextended. One answer is to help them learn how to delegate. Another is to formulate with your child a hierarchy of goals. Decide which are important and which are not. The tense young person can learn the art of selective relaxation.

Protect breaks. Young people who are establishing effective work habits should be made aware of the importance of a coffee break or lunchtime break.

The reason industrial organizations began to offer coffee breaks and lunch breaks was that studies proved that increased efficiency resulted when workers periodically rested during the workday. Short study breaks for students are equally effective. During this time of respite, light conversation or imagining a serene vacation spot can truly provide the body with time to regain its equanimity. People universally enjoy natural beauties in their surroundings, including lakes, waterfalls, hills, forests, canyons, and countryside. They enjoy the beauty of art, attend museums to lose themselves in a favorite picture. They can be caught up in music at a concert. They can be amused by the antics of animals, including those found in zoos. People who golf and sail mention experiencing of a suspension of time, the feeling that time is unimportant when they are sequestered with nature. These activities should be sought out by young people who often do not see it or find a balanced life.

Think yourself calm. Several cognitive-behavioral theorists and therapists have been testing ways of helping people examine the ways they can talk themselves into harmful belief systems. Serve as an advocate for your grown children by constantly asking, "Is this actually necessary? Are you indispensible? Are there other ways of viewing this?" The old cliche, "This too shall pass," can be calming.

Parents can show an adult child how to practice relaxation techniques. Have him or her imagine the setting where he or she is calmest. Have him or her practice imaging that scene when confronted with a stressful situation. Positive images help because we cannot hold two contradictory thoughts nor pay attention to two things at exactly the same time.

So turning one's attention elsewhere helps relieve stress.

Athletes use imagery to create a picture of themselves performing expertly. They use it to calm themselves and concentrate on the event. The mind in this way can be a powerful ally.

As maturing adults learn to reduce stress, their released attention can focus on other matters that contribute to psychological growth, e.g., the spiritual, the personal relationships providing natural highs.

Parents can help young adults by exploring and discussing ideas for stress-reduction aid. Ultimately, however, each maturing individual has to address the problem on his or her own and find a solution that is personally feasible.

Figure 15–1
Capabilities for growth released by stress reduction. As shown, growth accelerates after adversive or stressful events are successfully handled or avoided.

TABLE 15-2

OVERVIEW OF SUGGESTIONS

1. Change pace
2. Engage in sports, isometric exercises and other physical activity; change diet
3. Jealously guard leisure time, use it in a self-fulfilling manner
4. Practice relaxation techniques, biofeedback, to reduce anxiety
5. Brainstorm new ways, new resources from others' experiences
6. Worry
    a. set aside time to consider problem
    b. confide in someone
    c. seek information
    d. do something about source of problem, actively
    e. or, develop "balancing factors" (see #1–#5 above)
    f. seek professional help
7. Shorten the time involved with draining demands
8. Work on what can be controlled, accept that some things cannot, "go with the flow"
9. Keep a sense of humor, especially when so many horrendous things happen that it is absurd
10. Delegate, relegate
11. Protect relaxing coffee breaks, lunches, other respite
12. Visit a peaceful place
13. Think positively

CHAPTER SIXTEEN

ENDURING FAMILIES

"My daughter was married on my tweny-third wedding anniversary. After the ceremony my wife and I sat together comparing our marriages with those of our friends who have split up," said Mr. Callahan. "We decided that what we, and others who haven't split, do is share, spare, and care."

Mrs. Holmes glanced up from her pile of envelopes, fingers flashing as she continued stuffing brochures. "What does share, spare, and care imply?"

He laughed and reached into the box for more brochures. "We share each other's growth. We share everyday duties. We share gossip about our days, family, and friends at the end of each day. Some friends share it in louder voices as they grow older, but they still share. We spare time to do little things for each other and we also spare some time separately for ourselves. We care about what happens to concerns beyond ourselves: to our dreams, goals, surroundings, community, and loved ones."

SHARING

Human beings begin life in a family and, at best, through the bonding—the attachment—that takes place, learn the positive passion for living, the emotional support, and the sanctuary offered within a family. They bring their knowledge to their marriages. Even though the definition of "family" has enlarged to admit new forms in response to today's society, many families endure over time.

There are some basic, everyday ways in which partner and family cohesiveness can be achieved:

The adult partners in a family use words to convey their perceptions of events and emotions. Nonverbal behaviors also convey messages that enhance the relationship. As the initial sexual passion declines, the feelings of closeness and the strength required for commitment become stronger. Family cohesion stems primarily from a psychologically happy, healthy, married couple.

Couples who spend a few minutes each day listening with interest to their partners assimilate each other's point of view and can build toward consensus. Although wives (or female partners) are usually the ones who begin negotiating over severe differences, more and more husbands (men) are becoming sensitive to negotiations and compromise in building good relationships.

Gossiping about the day, about friends, and family enables each adult to picture the happenings in the other's day and to anticipate problems that might arise. This conversation also lets children understand what is proper, pro-social behavior toward other people and what their parents criticize as inappropriate.

Moreover, the discussion enables growing children to observe how problems are solved—sometimes by different solutions for each parent, sometimes by agreement or compromise. Families can use the practice of gossip to build positive feelings about family gatherings.

Mr. Callahan related, "Even though her children are small, my daughter has a practice of having everyone at the dinner table relating something amusing or something good that happened that day. It sets a positive tone for the rest of the dinner talk and the family looks forward to the pleasant gathering."

Men and women become socialized differently. They have learned to emphasize different components of life as important. Traditionally, little girls are talked to more by their mothers, learn to ask questions, focus on relationships between people, and give and receive feedback. Traditionally, little boys are taught to cover up emotions although compassion is admired in adult men. Boys are often taught to focus on practical matters. As today's families gossip, the sharing of male and female social behaviors becomes a means of adapting to each other's *modus operandi*. Both men and women benefit from opening and sharing the full range of human potential and can utilize their new options to achieve better relationships.

Sharing and negotiating may be more volatile in some families than others. But, there is a constantly strengthening trend toward egalitarian adult responsibility. Particularly among compatible couples, sharing is a hallmark of the enduring relationship. They discuss what must be done, what options may be chosen, what each other's needs are and how to meet these needs. Needs include time for companionship, for socializing, and for being alone. In fact, the use of discretionary time has become the most argued matter, replacing discussion of finances.

Unless two adults take time to perceive what each partner considers important, they are like two strangers occupying adjoining seats in a 747, flying together toward separate final destinations.

With the rapidly increasing number of dual-career families, negotiations about conflicting needs occur all the time. Being flexible enough to tender loving care when one partner is beset with deadlines underscores the need for ongoing sharing. Many men no longer feel burdened by having to deliver the achievement, status, and stimulation of the work-place to the rest of the family. Many women no longer feel deprived of opportunity to use their talents. In addition to these benefits of dual-career families is the sharing of financial burdens. However, in dual-career families, the scheduling of household tasks is difficult. Still, when both share the mundane chores, time is released for more important and satisfying pursuits. Similarly, sharing each other's achievements provides the impetus for accomplishing more. It helps partners grow and change and thereby stimulates new growth, as shown in Figure 6–1.

Enduring families frequently depend upon a common bond of spiritual belief. The bond gives them strength, particularly in times of crisis, and a linkage with the larger order of things. Spiritual sharing is unique to human beings. A congruent spiritual belief can affirm each person's view of life and its vicissitudes. Families need to be part of a link beyond themselves.

Rituals of organized religions are times for sharing and also for notifying the larger community of passages through important times of life. Other people are invited to share special events. For instance, the marriage ceremony declares mutual commitment to each other and to the world. Some commentators have noted that strong predictors of enduring marriages are (1) growing up in the same neighborhood and (2) having a formal wedding ceremony.

Those who share spiritual beliefs outside of organized religions likewise perceive strength and meaning in a common orientation. Their rituals also bind the group together.

Faith can be of great comfort in tragic times. Mr. Callahan explained, "When my son was killed in Vietnam, none of us would have put our emotions back together if we had not held each other and shared our deep faith. We were so torn individually by anguish and could not comprehend any meaning in losing him that way. Our faith gave us strength to handle the inexplicable, and we were able to share that faith with each other."

SPARING

Little things do mean a lot. Little things such as a touch, a smile, a quick glance of understanding, family jokes, rituals, and appearances at important events build closeness and commitment. Sparing time to call other family members and to pay attention to each other enhance the possibilities of growth in one's self and others.

Overwhelmed people, harassed people, have no chance to regroup and process perceptions. Many of the tactics for relieving pathological reactions to

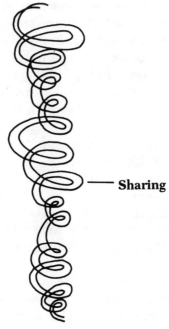

Sharing

Figure 16–1
Psychological growth spiral showing expanded possibilities through mutual involvement.

stress involve furnishing respite. Respite is a time-out procedure that helps heal beings bruised from too much bombardment of stimulation. Psychological growth also comes from quiet time, time to consider the whys and wherefores, the progress toward dreams, the happenings of one's day.

Mr. Callahan said, "We always paid a lot of attention to the kids—if they wanted it—until their bedtime. Then, we felt betrayed if they tried to pull some strategy for staying up longer. We are each other's most important person. The children are second. And that period after the children's bedtime was our private time. I liked to refinish furniture and my wife liked to cut things out with the jigsaw. We liked being in the same room, but we were comfortable with letting the other person be alone." The partners should set aside time to be together by themselves. Their relationship is important enough to plan regular time away from children. Shared passions for music, art, plays, camping, travelling add to the shared memories, the fun of being a twosome.

Friends outside the family constitute another psychological growth relationship. Friends are chosen; families are not. New things as well as different ways of handling situations can be learned from friends. Friends and relations enlarge the base of emotional support and provide wonderful ideas for new directions in learning and growth. This mutual support system has resources that go beyond what the two partners and their relatives can supply.

Strong families allow each person his and her individuality. Everyone is not expected to conform to what other members do. Instead, a treasure of riches is nurtured through individual talents, activities, characters, and goals. Spontaneity is present because of different interests and reactions. Partners and children enhance each other's growth by supporting differences, by participating in the other person's wishes.

Each family member's feelings, thoughts, and emotions are respected. Each can be him- or herself. "Each of my children has a different talent. Some in sports, some in the arts, some in club work. I have never let on that I do not understand soccer, because that is one kid's passion. I go to all the games and watch people run up and down the field. I cheer when the crowds cheer. When one of us is moody, we are treated differently because one wants to be kidded out of it, one wants to be left alone, one wants to get advice. We are different varieties and we are golden," Mr. Callahan declared firmly.

Competent children grow up in homes where parents permit even toddlers to try to do things their own ways, and intercede only to demonstrate alternative solutions to barriers. Children must grow toward independence, even during that in-between stage where parents think they have created adolescent monsters. Firm discipline is important in childhood but as children grow to adulthood they must learn self discipline. Presumably, the eventual product of successful parenting will be an independent, mature adult.

CARING

Throughout the span of the family life cycle, new decisions must be made and new ways of demonstrating care develop. Family life cycles are descriptions of tasks linked to the ages of children. Parents are children, have children, have grandchildren, etc., and they, too, participate in recurring cycles.

Some family structures will have no children, either by choice of the two adults or because they are infertile. Families with no children can focus on adult needs.

Most married and remarried couples—some gay and lesbian, unwed singles, and divorced single heads of households—have children. All usually have relatives and friends, sometimes from a different cultural background. All live in a work and social community. Caring is an important component of every meaningful relationship. In these relationships each person cares about another—about what happens, about the physical and psychological well-being of the others. Human beings have a predisposition to being social beings. Having someone care about what happens to us is one of our primary needs.

Caring contributes to a satisfying, memorable life. Most of us perform not only for our own self esteem but also because someone cares. Yet, it is important that our caring relationships have a sense of balance. Parents who are overly dependent upon their children, partners who try to drown their own individuality in that of their mates, will ultimately be unhappy, unfulfilled human beings.

Parents and partners who are *care*takers are also gatekeepers. With feedback and suggestions, they nudge both their own and others' goals along. First of all, they can help a child or partner voice an unspoken longing, help identify a goal. Second, they can help in expanding the breadth of alternative means for achieving the goal. Third, they can give balance to the weighing of possibilities in terms of the probabilities. Fourth, during these and subsequent steps, they can generate belief in the goal and support the ways and means of achieving it. Finally, if the goal needs re-examining, the mature, caring adult can assist in helping adult children or partners to view difficulties not as failures, but as one more set of results that did not work.

Showing this caring is of utmost importance, it reveals the respect and esteem each family member has for the others. People who are cared about are apt to realize consequences they cannot do more than speculate about alone.

Building toward a meaningful goal is different from acquiring material possessions. Taking the first steps to achieve such a goal is an intrinsically satisfying purpose.

The accomplishing of that purpose is shared by all who are party to the dream. In *Modern Man in Search of a Soul,* Swiss analyst Carl Jung said, "The meeting of two personalities is like the contact of two chemical substances: If there is any reaction, both are transformed."

Caring may even take the form of imposing tension: Helping channel tension to a fruitful outcome is qualitatively different from imposing demands. Caring people know the difference (see Figure 16–2).

Caring families may have to take a fresh look at problems of the daily routine. They, of course, expect each family member to carry out part of the chores of living safely and efficiently. Some routines can be traded around; some people prefer doing one task to another; some prefer doing them alone; others with help. Everyone in a home is better for contributing to the well-being and surroundings of the household.

Young adults should be taught to become involved in their communities. Several years ago, Harvard graduates were asked if they were involved in their communities and if not, why. Some of the men replied they were not involved because they did not know how to enter the community activities. Because of our mobile society, there is a need for solving local

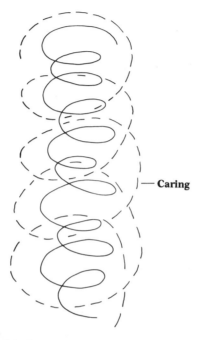

— **Caring**

Figure 16–2
The dotted-line psychological spiral shows how a flow of caring family members supports the growth of individuals.

problems with volunteer help; people can get involved with the needs of the larger community.

Neighborhood block groups, service organizations, and other socially-conscious groups have accomplished clean-up-fix-up campaigns, protection against crime, and political action efforts.

When a person becomes a volunteer, opportunities for satisfaction and self-renewal expand. Most newspapers carry ads for current volunteer needs.

Recreational centers always need coaches, youth groups always need leaders. Training is provided to help with transition. Sometimes a task force at an everyday institution (work, day-care center) leads to continuing individual efforts.

Religious groups and civic clubs seek new members and assistance in community efforts. The local governments often ask for people to apply for commissions and boards.

Young children like to particiapte in clean-up campaigns and volunteer money-raising efforts. Older children like to become part of the planning and work proposals. Parents can talk about the importance of these involvements.

Young adults sometimes prefer a one-shot project and sometimes want ongoing proposals toward which to devote their time; changes are often staggering when the idealism of youth matches a community need.

Caring about the larger community—extending one's capabilities—expresses compassion, teaches public relations, organization skills, reality testing, and conceptualization. Taking responsibility for the environment and for humanity is part of the highest order of psychological growth.

RECONSTITUTED FAMILIES

While the expanded definition of "family" has matched the changes in today's world and is accepted by professionals in marriage and family disciplines, many people still picture the ideal family as breadwinner father, homemaker mother, and two children. However, the last Census showed that only about fifteen percent of American families live under such circumstances.

Remarried divorced parents, married couples with no children (forty-nine percent of these in 1981), single-parent households, singles living alone and cohabitants (one in every twenty-five couples), are more typical than they once were. People are marrying later in life in the United States, and even later in Canada.

Reconstituted families present certain problems and questions:

- What role do I play in disciplining stepchildren?
- What is my financial obligation to stepchildren?
- How will the monies of two households be combined?
- How do we maintain the generational boundaries?
- How do we help the two oldest children from engaging in a power struggle to be the "oldest" and the two youngest from competing to be the "baby"?

As one can see, most problems center around the roles of the children.

A child whose parents are divorced will react differently depending upon his or her age. These reactions tend to disappear after a year or so. In the new marriage, the child may first welcome the new spouse, but then retreat from him or her as an in-

truder who is competing for attention. Part-time custody children arrive intermittently and impinge new
stresses.

After a divorce, preschool children may fear
their misbehavior caused the break-up of the parents,
or that the powerful mother sent the father away and
the same thing could happen to them. The young
child is still egocentrically linked to parents and may
use denial, imaginary worlds, and spiteful reactions
to playmates to cope with the separation. Early-
primary-school-age children may also become irrita-
ble and throw temper tantrums.

Children in upper primary grades manifest
intense immediate grief; they do not have the experience that adolescents have, nor the wider range of
activities and freedom that teenagers have at their
disposal. These upper-grade-school-age children
sometimes envision death, emptiness, and vulnera-
bility. Parents can assist children in trying to understand their dreams and nightmares and in identifying
feelings and understanding them as natural instead
of bad.

Children of a divorce may exploit one or both
parents or turn them into good guys/bad guys, with
the most absent parent being idealized. Often when a
new parent arrives on the scene, these issues become
exacerbated. However, with time, and discussion,
understanding such issues can be resolved.

In families where children were shielded from
parental anger, the adaptation is quicker and easier.
In turn, reconstituted families who have entered generational contact provide a setting that will contribute to adjustment. In addition maintaining generational boundaries is a helpful strategy. This means

that adults are treated as adults and children are treated as children.

As John Bowlby pointed out in his books, *Attachment* and *Attachment and Loss*, attachment behavior throughout life depends upon the infant's developing the capability to trust. This trust depends upon having consistent, dependable, and predictable consequences and actions. Learning to have faith in people begins early in life and is repeatedly accessed as new interpersonal situations arise. Children used as torpedoes against former spouses are greatly impaired in this.

Another issue is that of grandparents; grandparents do not want to be divorced from their grandchildren. Parents can help maintain these bonds. They are essential to children's healthy psychological growth.

Single-parent families, too, must treat children as children and not make children into sisters, brothers, husbands, or wives. Maintaining emotional equilibrium and acting as a good parent helps the children to be secure in their roles and to grow emotionally. However, it is also important for newly-single parents to adjust to their own roles and to reschedule parental priorities that arise as a result of jobs and single status. Friends and parents can allow the single parents to share anger, resentment, fears, etc. The person can adjust more quickly to new and often difficult responsibilities with such support behind them.

Along with problems of finances and overwhelming duties, single parents will have to help children field questions that may arise from outsiders: "What does your father do?" "My mommy is

head of the household; she's an office manager."
"Where is your father?" "He does not live with us."

The caring parent tries to help children cope and arranges as many safety nets as possible.

Real caring between partners demands negotiation and consensus. Respect for each other's opinions, heritage, and feelings enhances self-esteem.

Families have not only endured as an institution, but have also expanded forms and definitions. Through sharing, sparing, gesture, time and space, and caring, family members reveal underlying respect and appreciation. The resulting cohesiveness is reassuring to its members who feel sure: "If we drift apart, we'll eventually come back together."